For an organisation to win work they need to solve the needs of their clients. Sales is all about culture and Julia gets this. She has developed a repeatable system that focuses on getting culture right inside any organisation and helps your people grow. Where The Infinite Sales System has helped us is to understand that we have so many opportunities to learn from our clients about how we can be servicing them better by asking the right questions. Not only did The Infinite Sales System help our business improve its sales and systems but it also improved our people, the way our managers interact with our staff and the confidence our staff have in client facing conversations.

—**Tom Atkinson**, Director, Trainwest

Julia Ewert and her Infinite Sales System played a pivotal role in our journey from a small enterprise to a multi-million-dollar success story. Hosting the *Negotiate Anything* podcast, the #1 negotiation podcast globally, I have had the unique opportunity to interview the brightest minds in the industry. Having interviewed hundreds of people, I found Julia's expertise to be unparalleled. It was her system that we entrusted with our growth, and it delivered beyond our expectations. Her system isn't merely a set of sales tactics; it's a transformative force that has redefined the trajectory of our business.

Julia isn't just a brilliant mind, she's also one of the most genuine friends I've had the pleasure of knowing. Our journey began as professional colleagues, but over the years, she has become one of my closest friends. It's been an absolute joy to witness both her professional growth and to grow alongside her on a personal level.

—**Kwame Christian**, Founder & CEO, American Negotiation Institute

Julia's sales training made such a difference to my sales team and the way they spend time in the qualification and handling of objections. Such a unique perspective that helped us achieve more sales. I'm also personally using her techniques outside of work and, I have to say, it's worked every time!

—**Linda Grenfell**, Victorian Sales Manager, Development, Mirvac

Once you've been taught The Infinite Sales System, you'll find yourself asking, 'What would Julia do?' in most sales scenarios. What you need to know is that this is not any ordinary sales training. It's a system that if rolled out correctly across any business will produce results regardless of the personalities you have working in your business. This program is adaptable to anyone. If they are willing to get comfortable with being a little uncomfortable and follow the steps they will win more business and have a hell of a lot of fun doing it. Whether you think you are extremely experienced in sales or just starting out, this is the system for you. Attention all business owners ... implement this system into your business and you will convert more leads, win more clients and ultimately drive profit results.

—**Craig Kouimanis**, Head of Paragem

The Infinite Sales System is all about working smarter, not harder. It provides a crystal-clear path to convert more contracts, negotiate higher margins, and secure better clients. I love the straightforward, process nature of the system. By breaking it down you understand how small, deliberate actions add up to sales success. We have gained a rhythm for securing new members. Julia's advice and ideas have directly led to deals we wouldn't otherwise have won. Stop thinking about it and buy the book! Your bank manager will thank you for it.

—**Ashley McGrath**, CEO, CEOs for Gender Equity

Julia is a gifted professional, who maintains humility as a student of the craft of negotiation. She anchors her sales domain techniques in the same first principles of interpersonal communication and positive relationship development that we rely upon in the behavioral health domain. Her ethics, integrity, and commitment to her craft present high levels of personal and professional responsibility. If you are in sales AND you want to be a good human, read this book.

—**Andy Prisco**, Founder, Jumpstart Mastery

The Infinite Sales System is a timely reminder that a disciplined, repeatable approach to sales is always better than the ad hoc, personality-driven methods so often recommended. The lessons in this book offer increased sales, better client relationships and sustained business success for organisations of all sizes. The system is proven, now it's up to you, the reader, to implement the steps and boost your sales.

—**Dr Shaun Ridley**, Director, Ridley Insights

'What is sales?'

At the beginning, my aim was to help my sales team get better with negotiation. Instead, Julia trained us in a robust, practical, and soon very effective step-by-step sales process. We have learned a SKILL. At the end, it was a complete paradigm shift in the way we see and do sales.

'Everything is sales.'

—**Eddy Saleika**, CEO, Klaus Multiparking ANZ

FROM

PITCH

TO

PROFIT

FROM
PITCH
TO
PROFIT

How to Build Genuine Trust
and Achieve Business Success with
The Infinite Sales System®

JULIA EWERT

WILEY

First published in 2024 by John Wiley & Sons Australia, Ltd
Level 4, 600 Bourke St, Melbourne, Victoria 3000, Australia

Typeset in Tzimmes 10pt/15pt

© John Wiley & Sons Australia, Ltd 2024

The moral rights of the author have been asserted

ISBN: 978-1-394-26394-3

A catalogue record for this book is available from the National Library of Australia

Cover design by Wiley
Cover image © svetolk/Adobe Stock

Disclaimer
The material in this publication is of the nature of general comment only, and does not represent professional advice. It is not intended to provide specific guidance for particular circumstances and it should not be relied on as the basis for any decision to take action or not take action on any matter which it covers. Readers should obtain professional advice where appropriate, before making any such decision. To the maximum extent permitted by law, the author and publisher disclaim all responsibility and liability to any person, arising directly or indirectly from any person taking or not taking action based on the information in this publication.

CONTENTS

FOREWORD

In today's market, where consumers are increasingly wary of aggressive sales tactics, *From Pitch to Profit: How to Build Genuine Trust and Achieve Business Success with The Infinite Sales System*® presents a revolutionary shift in the business world.

The system stands apart from other sales' methodologies by rejecting traditional, high-pressure approaches in favour of building genuine connections based on trust and humility.

Author Julia Ewert describes an approach to sales that not only aligns with modern ethical business practices but one that also resonates deeply with clients seeking authenticity and real solutions to their needs.

Unlike conventional sales training that often results in temporary boosts, The Infinite Sales System provides a consistent framework for ongoing success.

Julia outlines an approach that goes beyond the simple act of selling a product or service. She explains that true selling is about understanding clients, fostering long-term relationships, and delivering real value. This approach ensures not just momentary achievements but a steady path to growth and profitability.

The Infinite Sales System is also a holistic view of sales as a journey of empathy, learning, and continuous improvement. It's not just a narrow approach focused solely on closing deals but a comprehensive philosophy that enhances the sales professional's ability to listen, empathise, and solve problems effectively.

The system transforms the sales role from transactional to relational, paving the way for more meaningful business interactions.

Adopting The Infinite Sales System is not just about improving sales performance; it's about embracing a new standard for ethical business conduct. It offers a blueprint for building lasting client relationships grounded in respect and mutual benefit.

For those serious about elevating their sales approach and contributing positively to their business's growth, this book is not a nice to have — it's a must have.

In an era craving authenticity and ethical practices, *From Pitch to Profit* is a beacon for those ready to lead the way in redefining success in sales and business at large.

> **Emeritus Professor Gary Martin** — Chief Executive Officer,
> the Australian Institute of Management,
> Western Australia

INTRODUCTION

First, thank you for investing in this book. ☺

Second, if this is the first sales book you've ever bought, you're steps ahead of the many who have gone before you, and tried all the things, before they came here. And by 'all the things', I mean they have tried learning from (stereo) typical sales gurus, attended countless sales training sessions, memorised a bunch of terrible scripts, copied some self-professing expert, or even tried changing their personality ... *all* the things!

If you happen to be someone who has *already* tried all the things, I'm confident that this will be the last sales book you ever need to buy, because this one aims to solve all your sales challenges once and for all.

This is what makes this book different. It is unlike any other 'how to do sales' book that you may have seen, or maybe already read, that still hasn't solved your problem — because now you're reading this book.

You're not alone in trying to find a process that works. One reason so many sales books are on the market is because large and small businesses all over the world are constantly trying to crack the code of sales.

I'm here to assure you, you can stop looking.

Why I wrote this book — and why you need it

Having worked in sales for 26 years now, I've seen and been involved in all sides of it — from the 'direct sales' (door-to-door) approach, through to leading sales teams for some of the largest companies in the world.

I've been in roles where I've either personally sold or managed teams selling a whole myriad of things — including kitchen knives (that's right, it doesn't get any more cliché than that!), hotel memberships, chocolate bars, dairy products, property, education, management services, insurance, telecommunications, lifestyle experiences, residential construction, dog treats, coaching services, sales training, and mentoring.

In addition, I've also been engaged to design and implement sales processes for companies selling marketing services, scaffolding, metal fabrication, mechanical parking stackers, software as a service (SaaS), consulting and auditing services, professional memberships, financial services, training, sticky labels, civil services, shipping and logistics, recruitment, organisational psychology, franchising, business broking, software and tech, architecture services, entertainment, crafting exhibitions, engineering, mining services, professional services, manufacturing, agricultural products, luxury camping tents, IT, interior design, healthcare and legal services.

So, it's fair to say, I've sold most things. I can even say I've sold used cars after upgrading my own vehicles over the years!

I wonder if your product or service features in, or is similar to, something in that list?

What I can share with you about all these different products and services, much to the surprise of many people, is that the baseline principles are the same. So a sales process for a company selling mechanical parking stackers is about 95 per cent the same as a sales process for a company selling marketing services. This is because a sales process is designed to engage and collaborate with another human, and most humans behave and are motivated in similar ways.

These days my company works with service and solution-based organisations, implementing my proven, holistic approach to sales. Refreshingly, this process allows people to simply be themselves, and is focused on bringing out the best in the person you're selling to. Who would have thought?!

Perhaps you are like many of my clients who, prior to working with me, invested plenty of money and countless hours working with various sales trainers and coaches or business strategists. You may have also tried all the marketing advice as well, such as investing in a new website, optimising your SEO, updating all your brochures and various social media accounts. Yet, after all these efforts, you're *still* not making the level of revenue you strive for.

With The Infinite Sales System®, I'm offering something different. And how I can assure you of this so confidently is because out of all the clients who have implemented this system, not one of them, to the best of my knowledge, has ever invested in another sales expert.

This system has stopped the bleeding, and these companies now have their own repeatable way of converting new business, in a way that feels right for them.

This book (and The Infinite Sales System) has been specifically designed to help professionals who either are not salespeople or, even if they recognise they are in sales, struggle to relate to the old-school tactics and tricks still being taught by some 'experts'.

I've written this book predominantly for professionals who don't see themselves as 'salespeople'. Perhaps your main employment role is as the technician, focused on the delivery of the services your business provides; however, you are also responsible for or tasked with bringing in or converting new clients. So you may not be in a full-time sales role, but the sales component does occupy a small (and heavily weighted) portion of your role responsibilities.

Or you might be in sales as a full-time role. While sales professionals following a traditional approach may be less likely to read this book (more on this later), if you're looking for a more modern approach, you can learn a lot here.

Warning: There is no magic ahead. Once you have read this book and familiarised yourself with The Infinite Sales System, you still need to do the work. The good news is that you will not need to change your personality type to become someone you're not — you don't need to transform into an extrovert and you won't need to learn any cheesy tactics or scripts. This book will teach you how to simply be yourself, and master sales at the same time. All in a repeatable way. How liberating.

It's time for a modern-day, holistic approach to sales.

One that is centred on humility, trust-building and human connection.

That time is now.

How to read this book

This book is not designed to be read like a novel — although the stories do promise to educate and entertain!

The best way to maximise your success from this book is to really engage with it. Grab yourself a highlighter and highlight the bits that resonate, fold the pages, get some post-it notes and stick them on, write notes directly on the pages and treat this book like a text book — this book is not designed to remain pristine! (If you're reading this as an e-book, use the bookmark, highlight and notes functions, or make notes on your phone or tablet.)

If anyone asks you to borrow this book, encourage them to buy a copy instead — not so I can make more books sales, but so they can also read the book in the same way, and add notes, highlights and page folds.

It might be considered sacrilegious to dog-ear a page in a book, but in my book (which is now *your* book), dog-ears are encouraged!

You may want to revisit certain chapters, as the principles become more evident as you progress. Feel free to do so! Read this book forwards, backwards, review chapters and read it from a randomly opened page. The lessons within will serve you as continual reminders, which will reward you with more sales success.

Frequently asked questions (FAQs)

After having worked in sales for so long, I know the kinds of questions that commonly come up. I've distilled the various questions I'm often asked — either directly by clients, or via social media — and included these as FAQs throughout this book, and especially as we get deeper into The Infinite Sales System.

As you make your way through, I'll throw in the FAQs in anticipation of helping you put your mind at ease, and solidifying your learning.

If by chance you have a question that I've not answered, I'd love nothing more than to hear it from you. You can contact me via the following:

- *Email:* info@juliaewert.com.

- *Website:* www.juliaewert.com.

- *LinkedIn:* Julia Ewert, MBA, FAIM.

Definitions

Throughout this book, I frequently use particular terms. So you're clear on what these terms mean in the context I use them, I've defined them here:

- *Client, customer*: What your prospect becomes once they have paid you money. Until such time that you actually see the money in your bank account (or, in Australia, perhaps they've raised a 'purchase order'), they remain a prospect.

- *Inbound prospect/opportunity*: Where a prospect or opportunity contacts you first. They become known to you, or come *inbound* to you, through a website enquiry, referral, word of mouth, trade show or other means or marketing efforts.

- *Outbound prospect/opportunity*: Where you contact a prospect first. This can be through 'cold calling' (don't worry, other options are available!), networking or directly going *outbound* and approaching a target opportunity in a warm way.

- *Prospect*: An opportunity you are in conversation with, or targeting for business. *Note*: Prospects and clients/customers are *not* the same, and I am very purposeful in my use of these terms. For the most part of this book, I refer to 'prospects', because this book is designed to teach you how to manage your prospects — who are ideally your future clients.

- *Sales, revenue*: Sales and revenue are the same things. In this book, I refer to both as 'sales' — which is by definition 'an exchange of goods or services for currency'. Irrespective of how you feel about doing sales, I'm asking you to draw a line in the sand and, from here on in, see sales in the same (hopefully, positive) light you see revenue.

- *Salesperson, business development manager (BDM), sales executive, account executive, business development executive*: Irrespective of the actual title, I amalgamate all these terms and simply refer to the 'salesperson'. After all, sales is one of the oldest professions in the world. If I advocate to 'fancy it up', then I too am shying away from what the role really is. It's 'sales', so let's all be okay with calling it that. We are all selling something — whether you are an engineer, lawyer, professional speaker, steel fabricator or trainer, if you are tasked with bringing in new clients, you're expected to be a salesperson as part of your role, in addition to your other field of expertise.

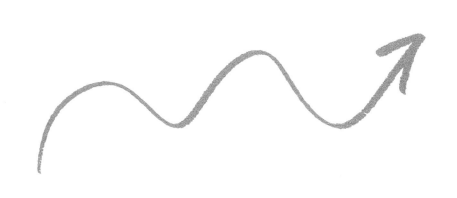

PART I

UNDERSTANDING THE IMPORTANCE OF SALES

Every time I hear someone compare doing sales to that clichéd used-car salesperson, a little part of me dies.

Too many sales 'experts' out there and too many old-school sales books are still teaching and spruiking sales techniques out of the 1970s. And even in this modern day, I'm still up against a large population who believe that 'sales' is a dirty word. Being told they need to do sales can make some people cringe and run a mile.

I wonder, is that how you feel about doing sales? Perhaps you see people working in sales as being pushy, aggressive, sleazy, used-car salesman-like, manipulative and cheesy.

The negative connection people have with selling often comes from decades ago practices associated with the high-pressure and aggressive techniques used by some to get people to buy, often under duress. Making people sign contracts by sliding a pen across a desk, or talking someone into buying something during a telemarketing phone call are examples that many people can relate to from decades past.

Plot twist: It doesn't have to be this way.

When done correctly, sales should feel conversational, calm, collaborative, agreeable and, dare I even say it, enjoyable — even for the most introverted of people.

In the chapters in this part, I run though why sales equals revenue, just who is best placed to make those sales, and what I see as the basics of modern-day selling. Finally, I introduce you to the process for doing sales the right way — using my signature program, The Infinite Sales System.

CHAPTER 1

REVENUE = SALES = BUSINESS

The function of selling is largely misunderstood. While it carries a perception that can make people squirm, many of those views have been carried forward from decades ago, when selling was very different from today.

Selling today is not about making someone buy something they don't want. Even if your product or service is the best thing since robot vacuums chased our pets, it's unlikely that any pressure you put on someone will be to the point where they are under enough duress to feel they must purchase. These days, consumers are too good at saying no and simply walking away.

But people — and companies — still struggle to understanding modern selling. Even though most of my clients are companies with turnover starting at $50 million (and much more), I am still regularly told by experienced CEOs and managing directors something along the lines of, 'Julia, you probably can't help our company, because we don't "do" sales'. When I dig a little deeper, they explain that this is because they aren't a sales company.

In my 26 years of business experience, the only word I believe you can interchange with 'sales' is 'revenue'. So to think that these large companies don't 'do' revenue — well, it just doesn't make sense, does it?

I have news for you, and it's all good: if you're doing revenue, you're 'doing' sales.

Years ago, I was selling to a large professional services firm. In my conversation with the managing partners, they acknowledged how much my system could help them and expressed how keen they were to progress things with me … But. They requested I make a change to my nomenclature — changing its name from a 'sales process' to instead be a 'business development process'. The partners argued it was unlikely their team would get on board with a program containing the word 'sales', because it would mean they needed to 'do' sales.

Of course they needed to do sales! How else did they think they would be converting new clients? This was supposedly, a modern-day, progressive company, but even they still carried the negative baggage associated with the word sales.

Plot twist: I did not change the name. ☺

Sales is revenue. Revenue is sales. It's all business.

Improving your sales approach to address your biggest challenges

In 2023, I conducted 49 interviews with CEOs and managing directors from my ideal client list. My objective was to learn about the biggest challenges they faced when it came to sales (revenue) within their organisation.

Surprisingly, I found the challenges these CEOs and managing directors outlined were no different to the responses I received in

2018 — and, I hazard a guess, will be similar to the challenges being faced 10 years from now.

In addition, I find these are the same challenges (to varying degrees) being faced by start-ups and smaller businesses, so these trends don't seem to discriminate between different business sizes and structures.

Here are the main challenges these businesses face:

- The vast majority of new business is won through the efforts of the owners, CEO or managing director (or other senior executives), which means revenue is too reliant on these individuals. These individuals then struggle to find a way to teach their front-line team to win business like they do.

- 100 per cent of the businesses have a specific group of team members who are experts in their technical roles, and are also expected to do sales or business development. Of these companies, 92 per cent admit to not investing 'sufficient' resources to equipping these members with sales skills. This means they were expecting their front-line team members to bring in new business, without teaching them how exactly to do it. This results in team members doing sales in different ways, all with varying degrees of success, which was impossible to measure.

- 94 per cent have experienced the frustration of working with the wrong type of clients. They have simply accepted any client, and committed to doing work either below what they are capable of or punching above their weight and trying to service clients too large for their capabilities.

- 60 per cent are more often than not competing on price, so they are often sacrificing margin to win deals. These businesses were all convinced that price is the largest differentiator they have, and that their clients will value this above every other factor in their decision-making.

- 100 per cent of these businesses are continually investing in marketing, but only 19 per cent are satisfied with the return on investment through sales conversions, which means they are losing far more opportunities than they aspire to.

- More than 70 per cent have pipelines beyond four months that they consider 'light on', and are relying on previous trends or 'hope' that business will perform as per expected. Their future pipelines are lacking opportunities, which leads to uneasiness and financial stress within the organisation.

- 100 per cent don't have a standardised way of doing sales across their organisation and are largely doing 'sales by accident'. They complain that this makes it impossible to predict revenue, measure performance fairly and train new team members.

- About 50 per cent of opportunities come through inbound leads, and 90 per cent of these businesses don't have an outbound method or process to approach and convert target opportunities. This leads to applying an approach of waiting, hope or even luck to bring in new opportunities, which is high risk.

- 62 per cent agree they are not using customer relationship management (CRM) systems proficiently to produce the business insights required to measure and proactively act on trends on sales activity, pipeline or forecasting, leading them to be flying blind.

- 67 per cent of those who have tried hiring business development managers (BDMs) are neutral on whether the investment has been worthwhile. Of those, 90 per cent still continue to use their technical employees to perform some sales duties.

- 92 per cent feel they struggle to articulate their value proposition or point of difference, leading to price being one of their biggest levers. They were all operating in competitive industries and using price to stand out. Not one of these businesses understands how their clients could see them as a more superior partner than their competitors.

- 100 per cent feel they are frequently caught up in operations or service delivery and don't prioritise time for networking, follow-up or prospecting.

Can you relate to these challenges, irrespective of the size or stage of your business?

Many of these companies had tried all the things to solve their sales challenges, and those who had engaged traditional sales trainers were still not confident their problem was being solved.

They had the right idea in engaging sales trainers; however, the whole model of 'sales training' was wrong — they just didn't know it.

Sales is about process more than training

When I started my sales consulting business, I was almost like every other traditional sales trainer out there. I had plenty of sales experience, had worked for large companies, and offered the same 'menu' of sales training topics.

How I *wasn't* like other traditional sales trainers was that I was female, I wasn't driving a Maserati or wearing a flashy Rolex, and I didn't subscribe to the 'rah-rah-jump-around' hype during sales training sessions that seemed to be more focused on mindset and motivation.

I did, however, start out in my business offering training workshops on generic sales topics — including building rapport, using open and closed questions, outlining features and benefits, handling objections and knowing how to close. Clients benefited from my training but, to be honest, probably no more or less than if they had worked with another sales trainer.

They did, however, keep having me back to cover other training topics, asking me to cover questions like, 'Now that we can ask the right questions, when do we ask questions?', 'When do we stop talking and when do we start selling?' and 'How can we talk about our offer in a way that makes us stand out?'

These questions lead me to the following conclusion: *sales training doesn't stop the bleeding, and instead of providing answers, it can often lead to more questions.*

Sales training, while essential, is like putting a bandaid on a severed limb. It won't stop the bleeding, but it can be helpful for a moment in time.

Consider a swimmer who wants to win an Olympic medal in the 100-metre freestyle. Particular skills are required to do this, such as correct stroke, kicking, breathing, diving and tumble turning. Let's assume the swimmer is highly skilled in every element of these individual aspects, which they have refined over a lifetime of practice through rigorous training. While they may be exceptionally well trained in kicking and tumble turns, this swimmer will never win an Olympic medal, or any medal for that matter, if they don't follow a process of deploying the right skills, in the right order.

Imagine the starting gun goes off and the first thing they do (while still on the starting block) is arm-stroke circulations. Then they turn their head side to side as if breathing in water. Then they dive in the pool and immediately deploy a tumble turn.

Although this scenario sounds completely ridiculous — obviously, the swimmer would need to dive in at the starting gun, and then use the correct stroke, kick and breathe — the lesson remains. They will never achieve much if they are lacking the process to win the 100-metre race.

Much like this swimming analogy, sales must follow a process. Training alone isn't enough if you:

- haven't got the right skills on board

- aren't highly competent in using these skills

- can't deploy the skills in the right order and at the right time.

In a sales environment, being great at asking questions, handling objections and closing isn't enough if you don't know how to describe your offer in a way that makes people need you, immediately. Similarly, having an exceptional offer isn't enough if you don't know when to start talking about it and when to tackle pricing objections.

Effective selling requires both the training *and* the system. With these two tools, anyone can do it — as long as they were willing.

This was how The Infinite Sales System came about. I scrapped my menu of individual sales training topics, and changed my entire business model to offer just the one service: a customisable, repeatable, end-to-end sales process.

Ironically (or not), this is the exact same system my company has used over the years to grow to the size we are now, with a team of certified facilitators of The Infinite Sales System, with the ability to service global clients.

We offer one product, for one price, and have never looked back.

Sales *training* is out; sales *process* is in.

Sales is as much a business necessity as marketing

Businesses are required to invest in countless considerations, both to stay open and to grow. Some of these investments include personnel, marketing, office premises, accounting and bookkeeping, product packaging, technology or office furnishings.

All these different elements require an investment of time and money, but few of them can create the same scale of impact as investing in a sales process.

When an economy gets hit, marketing personnel usually start to feel nervous about the security of their jobs. While salespeople may too feel added pressure, they are the individuals who can make a tangible difference to the bottom line of the business. By converting more sales, they are bringing in more revenue. Revenue keeps the business going and keeps people employed.

Yet, businesses readily sign up to invest time and money into marketing. You've likely heard comments like, 'We need a new website', 'We should invest in lead generation' or 'The business cards and marketing collateral all need updating'.

Companies then action these strategies and boast, 'Look at our amazing website!' or 'Check out these beautiful product brochures we've had designed!' And people marvel at the beautiful branding, the user-friendly website and the captivating copy and imagery on the brochures.

Can you recall a time that someone has said to you, 'Let me show you my amazing sales process?!'

Guess how many people spend time dreaming and strategising about having a repeatable sales process in their business? None. That's who. Well, aside from me! (Okay, and perhaps one or two others.)

Sales is often misunderstood — surprisingly, even by people working in sales. I often have to explain the difference between sales and marketing because, more often than not, people believe they are the same function. For years, people have incorrectly titled me as working in 'sales and marketing', whereas I have only ever worked in sales and have zero qualifications or experience working in marketing roles.

Sales and marketing share some common elements and common interests. One function cannot live without the other and each would struggle to survive in isolation. However, they also have very different deliverables or outcomes.

On one hand, we have marketing, which has a 'one to many' communication strategy. Marketers are delivering one message (or one story) to a large audience who are ideally their target market. Marketing strategies are based on customer expectations, research, development and promotion, and these strategies aim to create a brand identity and market awareness.

One of the deliverables of marketing is to generate 'leads' or 'prospects' — essentially to get people either to or in the metaphorical 'front door' of the business, which could be through a website or social media enquiry.

On the other hand, sales focuses on a 'one to one' strategy. While sales is more 'art' than 'science', much research and scientific findings are available on the psychology of why people buy and how they behave in purchasing situations. Salespeople rely heavily on interpersonal skills and sales techniques because their main purpose is to connect and communicate with somebody on a one-to-one basis.

If the output of a marketer is to produce leads or prospects, the output of a salesperson is to convert the prospect into becoming a paying customer.

Winding back to marketing, let's consider one aspect in finer detail: lead generation.

When people think about lead generation, they generally focus on producing *volumes* of prospects, rather than the *type* of prospect they should be targeting. Even if your company has an excellent marketing machine powering lead generation, it's possible that not every incoming lead will be the most ideal type.

Incoming leads are referred to as 'inbound' prospects or opportunities, and are those who come to you first, through referrals, website or LinkedIn enquiries, word of mouth, trade shows or calls to your front reception, for example. An inbound lead makes the contact with you first.

Outbound leads are those prospects or opportunities who *you* contact first, and who are possibly not even expecting your contact or your introduction.

Driving continually large numbers of high-quality inbound leads requires a large and continual investment in marketing time, effort and finance. Marketing of this nature doesn't have an end date and if you turn it off, the leads will also likely stop coming in.

A degree of hope also goes into marketing. (I can already hear all the marketing professionals out there telling me otherwise!)

What I mean by this is that once your marketing machine is in full swing, an element of hope enters the mix — *hoping* the leads come in, *hoping* they will keep coming in, *hoping* they are the right type, and *hoping* they convert into clients.

As a further qualifier, by no means am I intending to speak poorly about marketing investment. It's a necessary investment if you want your business to thrive. In my company, the marketing division is essential to my success, building my brand awareness and market reputation. Through these continued marketing efforts, I am able to convert high numbers of new clients.

However, even after all the effort and investment that goes into my marketing team and related marketing activities, my clients are still largely won through my outbound approach. For example, even when an inbound lead comes my way (through LinkedIn or through my website), *never* has such a lead been ready to immediately begin working with me. I still have to run through my sales process to convert them.

The two processes go hand in hand. Marketing efforts help them come my way, my sales process helps them convert.

In terms of driving leads, the good news is that if you convert at a high rate (anything over 70 per cent) and they are the right type of client, you don't need many leads, so you are rewarded with quality over quantity. This is also smart business.

When I talk about an outbound strategy, I'm not advocating for a traditional cold-calling approach. You can use many different methods to comfortably and genuinely approach companies you'd like to work with, all far from the stereotypical cold-calling you might fear.

Frequently, I hear prospects boast that all their new business comes through referrals, which means they don't need a sales process. I always reply with three (tongue-in-cheek) questions:

1. That's great! Tell me, when exactly are the next 10 coming in?

2. And exactly what kind of clients are they going to be?

3. And exactly how much revenue will they be worth?

While nothing is wrong with receiving referrals, relying on them too heavily is risky, and means that you just have to take what you can get. Before you know it, you can have many clients that aren't bringing you satisfaction and are draining your energy. You can find yourself thinking, *I'd love to have XYZ company as a client! I can't believe they choose to partner with our competitor.*

An 'inbound' strategy is what I call the 'waiting' strategy. You're waiting for the prospects to show their hand so you can engage with them. Solely relying on inbound leads can also become a dangerous strategy. It's unpredictable and makes it impossible to forecast your revenue.

An outbound strategy is also not without challenge. This requires a continuous investment of time and effort, and it's relentless. An outbound approach is a task that never comes to an end, kind of like your email inbox — the more you get on top of it, the more that seems to flood right back in!

When talking with companies caught up in and focused on client delivery, I often hear, 'We don't have time to do sales'. The best balance is a hybrid strategy, comprising both inbound and outbound prospects. In this kind of approach, your marketing team are driving brand awareness and general marketing activity, and your existing team are given the skills and process to do some sales.

This way, you don't need to hire an expensive full-time salesperson. Instead, a small portion of each existing team member's time is spent on sales, which when done with competence, will reward you with far greater sustainable results across your company.

As the little girl in the famous taco television commercial once professed, in her attempt to settle the polarising debate about soft shells or hard shells, *'Por qué no los dos'* — 'Why can't we have both?'

CHAPTER 2

WHO SHOULD DO SALES?

I have an engineering client who once hired a full-time business development manager (BDM — otherwise known as a salesperson) to help them supercharge their efforts in converting new clients. This was the first time they had hired for such a role; previously, sales was only an 'inbound' activity where the company took orders as they came in. They also didn't have much of an 'outbound' focus because the team were often caught up in delivery of the services. (Jump back to the previous chapter for more on the difference between inbound and outbound leads.)

When I commenced working with the team, the BDM was a new employee, so the team were all going through my training together. This salesperson brought with them more than 16 years in sales experience, across various industries, and the company was thrilled to have secured such a wonderfully experienced new team member.

In my early work with this team, however, I began to see that while this salesperson was experienced, they also carried a lot of bad habits. Their experience was in more high-volume, transactional sales, where the business relationship was not as important and the sales cycle was quick. The sales skills they demonstrated were not aligned with building trust first, before any attempt is made to sell anything. They were harder to coach and were the last person in the team to learn the recommended techniques or master the skills. The sales skills they did have were not strong and were more dependent on trying to become best friends with prospects.

They preferred to go and do their own thing, rather than to follow the sales process that the company had invested in. All that hard work came undone. They were hard to coach and less open to new ways of operating, and because they had been in sales for 16 years, they had an attitude of knowing it all already!

This is not too dissimilar to other salespeople I have worked with. Companies often don't know what to look for when recruiting salespeople, and they frequently face challenges around how to structure sales roles or manage salespeople for optimum performance. This leads to making risky (and expensive) hiring decisions, and being left with poor performance and a feeling of failure.

In this chapter, I look at who might be the best at sales in your business, comparing dedicated salespeople with front-line experts. First, though, let's quickly consider the two main categories of business, and how the category your business is in might influence your sales approach.

Two types of businesses

I have observed two main categories of businesses: traditional sales businesses and non-traditional sales businesses.

Traditional sales businesses are more likely to be selling high-volume and (sometimes) lower ticket item products and services. They operate more on a transaction basis with their 'customers' (infrequently called 'clients'). They are more likely to have shorter decision-making time frames, which require less effort, but a large marketing investment to keep the brand awareness top of mind. Examples of these kinds of businesses include retail, telecommunications, real estate, software as a service (SaaS) platforms, property, insurance and, yes, car sales businesses.

These businesses readily 'sign up' to knowing they are in sales, and a strong sales focus and sales culture exists within the company. In many cases, they have a team of salespeople, tasked with making sales. The sales team usually have sales-related KPIs or targets, and the salespeople are in-tune with their numbers, targets and performance.

Non-traditional sales businesses are more likely selling lower volume, high-ticket item products and services. Given the nature of the high value of these items, the relationship these businesses have with their prospects and clients is much more important than a transaction. These prospects are high stakes, and can take a lot of effort and time to convert. These businesses likely don't invest as much in marketing, and instead rely heavily on referrals and word of mouth for new opportunities. Examples of these kinds of businesses include accounting, legal, financial services, marketing, IT, HR consulting, training, engineering, technology, healthcare and manufacturing businesses.

These kinds of businesses rarely have a sales team, although they may on occasion employ a BDM to help them win new business. They usually rely on their existing front-line team to convert new clients when enquiries come through the door, with this same team then also being responsible for delivering the client work (as the accountants, engineers, architects or lawyers, for example).

Surprisingly, many managers and leaders in these non-traditional sales businesses do not associate themselves with being in sales. It seems to be a foreign concept.

For too many people, the thought of 'doing' sales seems to make them think they're being asked to overhaul everything and step back to the year 1980.

Consider for a moment, which of these categories do you most align to in your current role? How about your previous roles?

Through my experience in working with these types of companies, I've also seen how different the employees are from those in traditional sales businesses. Although they are largely unfamiliar with the concept of formalising and structuring sales, the individuals are often highly educated and qualified to work in their field of expertise — and it's encouraging to continually hear how fascinating they find the learning experience of sales.

Many of the individuals begin with the same (negative) idea of sales; however, when I explain sales is more about trust building, humanised principles, humility, connection and honesty (not words you often hear associated with sales skills), they always embrace these ideas.

They also respond well to the integration of negotiation skills in the process. As a new set of practical skills that they can use daily, negotiation skills give them an edge and make the topic more interesting for businesspeople than simply 'sales'. For most of them, this is brand new information and they are always actively engaged in listening, learning and practising.

This is almost a 'greenfields' learning environment, where we have a blank slate to work with, and don't have to deal with egos, arrogance or the 'we've heard this all before' attitude, frequently found in traditional sales companies.

Importantly, these non-salespeople love it! I am still constantly being told how surprised clients are to be enjoying sales, and of the wins they have. They are consistently enjoying the success of engaging in conversations with prospects and converting more qualified clients, with higher margins and faster sales cycles. Everyone wins. In fact, a logistics company I worked with had all three directors of the business 'do' sales themselves for 12 months because they were enjoying it so much and were achieving so many wins!

These days, these are the types of businesses I work with, and I leave the 'traditional sales businesses' to be served by other professionals.

Who are the most successful salespeople?

When most people think about the perfect salesperson, they still picture someone who talks a lot or has a strong, extroverted personality. Indeed, if someone talks a lot, they're commonly branded with, 'You should work in sales! You could sell ice to Eskimos!'

This perception of who makes a good salesperson couldn't be more incorrect. Instead, the technical expert or the introvert within your business can be a prime candidate for this role (if they are willing) because the requirements are learned skills, not necessarily 'natural-born' skills, as is often believed.

The stereotypical salesperson tends to be an extrovert and highly sociable. My experience has shown me that many of these types of people end up being highly *ineffective* at sales because they:

- tend to talk more than they listen

- are highly transactional, rather than strategic

- like to be the hero of the conversation, rather than letting someone else share what is important to them

- are dominating

- can be arrogant

- can be difficult to manage

- can be hard to coach

- have high ego.

Indeed, the opposite of these traits are usually more successful. This means a highly effective salesperson is often someone who is:

- great at listening

- asks insightful questions to draw out what is important to their prospect

- strategic and tactical

- humble

- purposeful and deliberate

- open to learning.

This is what makes a great salesperson.

Dedicated salespeople versus front-line workers

Some companies choose, either by design or default, to have a business development team or business development person. Others, like many of my clients, choose instead to leverage their existing resources and capabilities.

Either way, focusing on the key function of sales is important, and companies that don't have that focus often risk attracting the wrong types of clients, creating long buying cycles and unoptimised margins.

But which approach is better? Having dedicated sales and business development roles, or equipping your current front-line team (who are not salespeople) with sales skills? As I've mentioned, many managers and leaders resist this second option. (To really emphasise this point, if I had a dollar for every time a managing director told me, 'Julia, we don't do sales', I'd have enough money to buy my kids the actual-size working garbage truck they've been badgering us about for years.)

They (the managing directors, not my kids) go on to tell me that their front-line team are excellent lawyers, engineers, consultants, accountants, technicians or whatever, and that they are not really cut-out for doing sales. At this point, they usually ask about hiring a dedicated person — someone specifically hired to do sales full-time.

Hiring someone specifically for the role of sales is an excellent idea. You'll have someone focused full-time on hunting for and converting new clients. It will be raining new clients and they will all be amazing!

Plot twist: These people are hard to find — very hard, in fact. They are also very expensive, and they can also be very hard to manage.

Many countries and industries go through cycles of massive labour shortages, and if the challenges of a labour shortage aren't enough, then finding a specialist who possesses a high level of competency in finding and converting high-quality clients in your specific industry is also not going to be easy.

Hiring specifically for sales

I had a meeting with a prospect who ran a large manufacturing business, and they shared that their plan was to double revenue by hiring a business development manager. I enquired about how exactly this person was going to do the sales and secure this revenue. They told me, 'We will just teach them what we do, and then they will go and get the sales.'

I then asked them a few follow-up questions:

- Where will they be getting the sales from?

- What process will they follow?

- How will you use KPIs or measure them?

- How will you know in the job interview if they are going to be successful in this role?

These questions (and the right answers to them) are often largely misunderstood by leaders in non-traditional sales businesses when hiring for this specific role. These companies often make a (expensive) recruitment decision based on how many years' sales experience the person has on their resume; and if they seem like a decent human with a good personality. Indeed, the common conclusion I've heard from recruiting managers can be summed up as follows: 'This person has a great personality, lots of experience in sales and business development, and our customers will really like them!'

However, this kind of statement comes with three huge red flags:

1. Engaging well with *clients* is a very different skill to bringing in new business from *prospects* where the relationship hasn't been established.

2. Hiring based on personality is not an indicator of sales ability.

3. Their sales skills haven't been tested in the interview so whether they can find and convert new business is unknown.

According to *The Challenger Sale* by Matthew Dixon and Brent Adamson, the vast majority of companies hire the same type of salesperson. Unknowingly to them, this person is often the least effective type of salesperson.

Is a dedicated salesperson worth it? Indeed — *if* you get it right, because these people are worth their weight in gold. But get it wrong, which is extremely common, and you've got an expensive liability on your hands.

Because getting it right is often so difficult, and even more so now with the talent issues everywhere, your sales approach and process is also difficult to scale, because you are dependent on finding 'unicorns'. Hence, this approach is best left to businesses that have very clearly defined BDM roles, and reliable access to a pool of talent.

In an ideal world, where high-quality labour resources were readily available, hiring someone specifically to work on new business would be an excellent strategy. However, in the real world, you may need a different approach for your business.

Using your front-line team for sales

What about leveraging your current front-line team? Are they going to be as effective?

Using your existing team to bring in sales has some great potential benefits. For starters, they already know the business and the work, and they can outline how their company best services their clients. They are also technically strong when speaking about the complexities of the services they can provide, and they are armed with solid case studies and stories of their own. Your existing team know what it takes to deliver the client work, and what kind of clients are great clients for your company. The depth of these insights can be difficult for a dedicated salesperson to capture and pass on.

Your front-line team can easily transition between meeting a new prospect and delivering them the work. They can also transition between delivering the work and continuing the conversation for even more work on other projects for that same client.

The biggest challenge for your existing team lies in their lack of skills to prospect for business, follow up with prospects and, importantly, convert the business. However, the highly effective — and scalable — solution to addressing this challenge is to establish a best-practice sales process that guides your team through the journey.

Add on some upskilling in the key skills they can use in that sales process, some ongoing coaching and training, and you'll have implemented an effective, scalable and more risk-mitigated 'revenue-machine' for your business that enables your best people to be even better.

FAQ

Q: But, Julia, how do I decide?

A: Whether you hire a dedicated salesperson (or team) or use your front-line team for sales is your decision, but it should be based on effectiveness of sales (and cost-effectiveness), scalability and structure. In addition, both options still require a sales process to follow.

Given the tough labour market, and the risk associated with full-time salespeople, gearing your existing team to step up and conduct some sales activity (for a portion of their time) could be the perfect option for you.

You've got business development professionals right in front of you! I don't know about you, but I love solutions that are hiding in plain sight.

CHAPTER 3

BASICS OF MODERN-DAY SELLING

In the next chapter, I introduce you to the underlying principles and core aspects of The Infinite Sales System. In the chapters in part II, we then dive head first into the detail of the system, running through the process step by step.

Before we get to this detail, I first need to outline some sales fundamentals. I see these foundational elements as being integral to any sales approach, regardless of the industry your business is in. Understanding them will help you be more successful as you learn — and start implementing — my sales process and The Infinite Sales System.

If you wing it, you won't win it

Some of the most popular business books follow a common methodology, in that they present case study after case study to capture the common traits found in the most successful companies across the globe.

One such example is Michael Gerber's *The e-Myth Revisited*, where he argues that the smartest companies in the world operate their businesses in a highly systemised, or process-oriented, manner. Rather than simply making it up as they go, Gerber suggests that in these companies, 'The system runs the business, and the people run the system'. In other words, the process or the system is what should be developed and followed, and then humans should be hired to implement those steps.

After all, hiring people and then telling them to make it up as they go, or 'just do what you think is the best way', is a terrible strategy.

Imagine a company that produces glass bottles hired seven factory workers and told them, 'The machines are over there. Just go and do your best'. Say each of these new hires then went about doing their best — some had great ideas, some wanted to skip steps, while some followed the same steps but in a different order. What can you imagine happening?

The number of bottles produced per hour would be unpredictable, the end result might not even hold any liquid, the bottles may be different shapes, and they might look fine, they might look terrible or they might be too brittle. These results make it impossible to forecast production, and the company's market reputation would be negatively impacted because of the poor quality and lack of consistency.

Let's look at McDonald's as another example. Whether you love or loathe their menu, their business model is one of the most successful in the world. McDonald's aren't in the hamburger business; they are in the 'systems and procedures' business. When you buy a franchise, what you're really paying for is their operating manual, which tells you exactly how to make the burgers that produce your revenue.

Can you imagine what would happen if McDonald's sold a franchise to someone and just told them to make the fries and the burgers the best way they could? The outcome would be unpredictable, the business revenue would be difficult to forecast and the customer experience would be hit and miss. As Michael Gerber states in his book *The e-Myth Revisited*:

The system runs the business, and the people run the system.

This is not at all an unfamiliar concept. Businesses commonly have highly systemised internal processes, such as how they recruit and onboard new team members, ensure accounts are paid on time, deliver their products and services, or conduct their marketing function. The most successful companies in the world are very unlikely to be making all those processes up as they go.

How your company does sales should be no different. In my experience, however, many companies are indeed making it up as they go. They are doing sales by accident — and I've learned that if you wing it, you won't win it.

Does your business have a 'Frazer's Engineering way' or a 'Brad Marcus Accounting Advisory way' or a 'Matisse's Legal Group way' (or however this process could be branded) of converting new clients?

Without a standardised way of converting new clients, you risk working with just any clients — including the ones who are less than ideal, who take up a lot of time and eat away at your margins. You also risk not being able to accurately forecast your business, so knowing the right time to make investment decisions or budget cuts becomes more difficult.

Lacking a standard sales process also means your team members are all trying to convert new clients in their own way, which is highly inefficient. Then, when sales (revenue) are down or up, it's impossible to find patterns to analyse (outside of market conditions).

If your team are all following the same process and one person experiences a blockage in their pipeline so to speak, it's easier to troubleshoot solutions because you have a pattern of data to work with.

If seven people are all doing different things, finding patterns is impossible! A *'Your Company* way' of doing sales means that you have a consistent prospect experience, and you'll find sales easier to manage and measure.

I should qualify an important point here: just because your process is repeatable (and I've used a manufacturing example here), this doesn't at all mean your process is robotic. It's the complete opposite. With a repeatable process, your people can be *more* human, because you're able to use a highly engaging way to interact and convert new opportunities.

Having a repeatable sales process in my company means that when I forecast sales for the quarter, my results generally end up with the exact dollar I predicted three months prior. This means I know when I can make large investments, bring on new team members, experiment with marketing activity, or take time off.

This repeatability also means that when I cross paths with a large (lucrative) opportunity, I don't have to reinvent the wheel. I just do exactly the same as what I do with every other opportunity, which makes for an efficient system.

The system (sales process) runs the business, and the people (your technicians or front-line staff) run the system.

Negotiating is more important than selling

Much like many of the other misunderstandings covered so far, these also exist when using the terms 'selling' and 'negotiating'. Do you view these two terms as the same? Are they interchangeable?

Selling, simply by definition, is 'an exchange of goods or services for currency'. It focuses more on the transaction of the interaction between parties, and is usually one-sided.

We are all consumers who buy things for ourselves, and have been sold to by salespeople. Often we know the sales element is coming our way when we hear the pitch, which is all about the product, the price, the features and benefits, and why you should want it. Selling should really be a short part of this interaction, because it's usually the point you're being talked at, or presented to about the product or service.

As an example of good practice, when I'm selling my services to prospective new clients, our meeting is booked for one hour. The 'selling' part of that meeting comes at about the 45th minute, and it goes for about four minutes, rarely longer. You might be wondering at this point, 'What on Earth are you doing for the remaining 56 minutes then?' Stay with me ...

Negotiation is 'a discussion aimed at reaching agreement', and is more about partnership. It's about the details surrounding what could constitute an agreement, covering what is important to everyone involved in the discussion, how we will agree, and what the terms and conditions might be. It is a far more in-depth discussion, and also far more insightful than simply just selling.

 Sales is more about 'me', while negotiation is about 'us'. Sales is much more transactional, and negotiation is much more tactical.

To explore this idea in more detail, let me give you some real-world examples.

A new way: Negotiation and sales skills

As an avid reader, 95 per cent of books I read are business-related, and about 80 per cent of those are negotiation books. What began for me as a passive interest in a negotiation book I read years ago, led to reading dozens of others, and I'm now a proper nerd for the topic of negotiating.

I'm also resourceful, and this particular characteristic has always served me well. I'm often prepared to do what others couldn't be bothered with, or haven't thought about doing. These things are far from earth-shattering ideas because I'm not at all a creative person. So rather than coming from any grand and ingenious ideas, my success comes more from the persistence and discipline I apply.

After reading some of these early negotiation books, I thought to be resourceful and contact the individual authors to share what I liked and learned from them. Even today, I continue to be surprised at just how available many authors are to their readers. And I continue to be grateful for having met many of them.

I've met Harvard negotiation professors, police negotiators, crisis negotiators, FBI agents, hostage and terrorist negotiators, de-escalation experts and corporate negotiators, and almost all have become personal or professional friends of mine. Many of them have introduced me to others and welcomed me into advanced negotiation training sessions, and I'm often one of the few who isn't from a law-enforcement, crisis, or first responder background.

Something fascinating I've learned from these experts and training sessions is that when the FBI is conducting large-scale dangerous hostage negotiations, they consistently achieve about a 95 per cent rate of peaceful resolution. Now in the sales world, that's a pretty impressive conversion ratio!

That statistic continues to blow my mind, and it always surprises people when I share this. These are professionals who are negotiating with some of the most dangerous people on the planet, and they are almost 100 per cent successful.

Furthermore, because I know these professionals, I get to ask them about how they achieve this. What did they say? What did they do? What process did they follow? And I'm constantly blown away by the realisation that the exact same skills and techniques that the FBI use in hostage and crisis negotiations, can be used in a repeatable sales process, to help companies convert more qualified contracts, increase their margins and win more negotiation conversations of their own — and without any violence!

As an example of how these negotiation skills cross over, let me share a story from a now-retired NYPD negotiator friend of mine,

Jack Cambria. Now, in the negotiation world, Jack Cambria is not just 'kind of a big deal'; he's probably one of the biggest deals, in terms of his police negotiation experience. To put my meeting Jack in perspective, imagine how some people might feel if they were going to meet a Kardashian. That's how I felt when I was about to meet Jack.

Another professional colleague and good friend of mine in the United States is Andy Prisco, who has decades of experience changing lives through his application and teaching of verbal de-escalation. Andy is a true master of his craft. He created a high-performance verbal de-escalation and negotiation skills training group, of which I am a proud to be a founding member of.

His program — Jumpstart Mastery — is where I go to learn about how negotiation skills can change the world, and it's also the place I go for training to keep my skills and knowledge on this topic tiptop.

Andy has curated a group of some of the sharpest crisis and negotiation minds on the planet, and I'm continually humbled to be included. Through this group, I've met some professionals who I know will be lifelong friends.

When I found out that Andy knew Jack Cambria, I asked for an introduction. Jack and I weren't able to meet for several months and so we exchanged emails in the meantime to get to know one another. (Jack later told me that after Andy introduced us over email, he did what any good cop would do and researched online to become all expert on me before he responded! I'm thankful to Google and the SEO Gods, because Jack decided to meet me, phew!)

In one of our email exchanges, Jack told me something that would forever change the way I thought about sales and negotiating. He said that we were pretty much in the same job. 'How do you figure that, Jack?' I curiously enquired. Jack Cambria is a 34-year police veteran who retired as the New York City Police Department's longest-standing Hostage Negotiation Team Commander. What could he possibly have read about me that led him to think we did the same job?!

He shared that the sooner his team were able to wrap their heads around the fact that they were salespeople, the more effective they were on the job.

Still, I was puzzled. 'How do you figure that, Jack?'

He went on to tell me that he, too, was a salesperson. Now, I frequently talk about the fact that we are all in sales to some degree, but for some reason this seemed like too much of a stretch.

I wonder, though, can you see Jack's logic here? I'd love to ask you to think about this for a brief moment and, maybe, it will change the way you think about sales as well.

Riddle me these two questions. If Jack's police negotiation team are actually salespeople, as he says they are:

1. What is the product or service they are selling? (What are they trying to get people to 'buy'?)

2. Who are their 'clients'? (Who are they selling this product or service to?)

Answer:

1. They are selling jail time.

2. Their clients are the hostage takers.

Here is the story Jack told to me to explain these two points:

> An individual was standing on the rooftop of a NYC high-rise, threatening to jump some 14 stories to his death. He had just brutally stabbed his live-in girlfriend and had retreated to the roof as the police were closing in on him. When I got to the roof he told me that he would rather die than go back to jail.

> He told me he was a heroin addict, a high-school dropout and had no skills (earning his money by doing street robberies). So he felt that he was better off dead.

Now the sales pitch:

> After listening, and learning a bit about him, I said that in his case, maybe jail was not a bad option for him.

> To his first point: He was a heroin addict. In jail, he would be placed in the infirmary and taken off the drug; detoxified.

> His second point: High-school dropout. He could attend classes in jail and pass his GED (General Educational Development) tests, equivalent to a high school diploma. He could maybe even achieve a college degree.

> His third point: No skills. He will learn skills in jail, such as working in the kitchen, carpenter shop or metal shop, so that when he got out, he would be in a much better position to become a productive member of society.

> He looked at me and said, 'I never thought about jail in that way!'

> Sales deal closed: he came off the building's edge and was taken into custody.

Using the sales analogy, the sooner Jack's team could have the hostage taker or offender agree to accept ('buy') jail time, the sooner the negotiation would peacefully resolve, and the more effective his team were.

That story has forever solidified to me how intertwined the disciplines of sales and negotiating are.

As a reflection of this, The Infinite Sales System is a sales process based on world's best practice in sales process *and* negotiation skills, giving it a higher level of professionalism than simply offering sales skills, which are primarily designed to simply transact.

This system is designed to help you reach levels of true partnership with your clients, which I'm sure you will find far more rewarding.

Discipline always wins

After the first couple of sessions, a brand new client recently said to me, 'Julia, this system is great so far, but the team are wondering when the magic is coming.'

In another example, a different client once shared with me that their team weren't enjoying a particular part of my regular training — where they were tasked in each session with practising a particular (advanced) negotiation technique. When mastered, this technique allows an individual to respond in a warm and open way when someone disagrees with you or objects to you. The feedback from this client was that the team felt they had nailed this technique and didn't want (or need) to keep practising it for a portion of each session.

During my next session with the team, I thought to test them on this, without sharing that I was privy to this feedback. I told them I had conducted some market research and concluded that their offer was priced too high. I advised them to seriously consider a discounting strategy to gain some quick market share. I then went on to suggest that some of their competitors had a higher quality offer and were more experienced in their service delivery.

Then I stopped talking.

I had barely finished my last sentence when I saw their body language change. With frustration in their eyes, they then verbally attacked me with phrases like, 'We are much more experienced than our competitors!', 'There is no way we are going to drop our prices!' and 'How can you even suggest we are not the highest quality!' The reactions came in thick and fast.

I stayed present, in silence, and just listened.

Eventually, when they had finished, I changed the topic for a brief moment and asked them how competent they thought they were in that particular technique, which we had spent much time on, and which was designed to help them when anyone objected to them or their offering.

It took one team member to speak first, and they asked me with a smile, 'You've just made that scenario up, haven't you?'

The others then quickly caught up, with another team member asking, 'You just told us that to see how we would respond, didn't you?'

And someone else said, 'You haven't conducted any customer research on us, have you?'

Then they realised: 'And we didn't use the technique, did we?'

Nothing beats the discipline of following a process *and* the discipline of practising.

The best athletes in the world still spend countless hours on even the most basic (and even boring) of techniques. They do the same simple, fundamental exercises over and over again, until they can execute these exercises, perfectly, without thinking much about it. This is called 'muscle memory'.

In my younger days, I spent many years in the sport of gymnastics — first as a gymnast, and then as a coach. Gymnastics can be quite a dangerous sport and with one wrong move, lifelong injuries can occur. In the beginning, gymnasts spend more time missing a landing or getting a skill wrong than they do getting it right. As coaches, we spend numerous hours teaching the athletes how to land safely, preparing them for when they 'miss' a skill. We get the athletes to practise falling safely and missing a landing safely. We do this over and over again, so that if they do accidentally miss a big skill, and they only have a split second to get themselves to safety, then they can do so without thinking.

Muscle memory is a huge part of any sport, and is not just about safety. In a simple game of tennis, muscle memory allows the player's body to shift the right way when a backhander is coming their way, without having to think about their foot stance or hand grip. It allows athletes to respond the right way, at the right time, without having to lose time or brain power in conscious movement or overthinking.

Muscle memory is only built from repeating the same skills or techniques hundreds, thousands or even millions of times.

 In the sales arena, muscle memory allows you to respond (not react) in the right way, at the right time, with the right skills and techniques.

Mastering these skills requires repetitive practice and discipline.

Imagine if the FBI hostage negotiators I mentioned earlier in this chapter decided to just turn up at the hostage situation and launch straight into yelling at the hostage taker. Or they thought they could simply ignore everything the hostage taker says. The situation would take a turn for the worst fairly quickly.

These professionals are more disciplined than most, so is it any wonder, then, why they are able to achieve such a high level of success?

I've taken this concept of discipline and made it one of my company values. The value of discipline helps my team focus on keeping things simple, rather than reinventing the wheel, and we focus on what we already know works. For you and your team, discipline means 'doing the things' — following, and practising, the process outlined in this book. Don't skip the steps, and resist the temptation to add extra bits in. Just keep it simple.

 **Discipline always wins.
Just do the things.**

Play the long game

When the FBI is involved in the big-scale hostage situations that tend to make the news, two teams turn up: the FBI tactical team and the FBI negotiation team.

The tactical team might have 20, 50 or even 100 people in it, and these individuals are armed with guns, tear gas and stun grenades. These team members are recruited with specific characteristics in mind — they have exceptional self-control and are action-oriented. They cannot be seen to hesitate to act when a situation arises. They are unlikely to want to stay for long, and instead want to go in, get the job done, and get out.

The negotiation team are also a 'team', rather than just a singular person (contrary to popular belief). This team could be made up of 20 people, or even more, and also turn up with weapons. Do you know what they are?

They are the same weapons also available to most of us: ears and a mouth.

The team are equipped with listening devices. While one person communicates directly with the hostage taker, most of the others are allocated 'listening orders'. Individuals are ordered to listen for specific aspects — for example, signs of distress, children, how many people might be inside, the mood of the hostage taker, the emotion behind the words, and when they might become animated, angry, talkative or considered.

Much like any other situations in general life, one person can often have a view on what they think they heard someone say or imply, while someone else can have a completely different view. It's hard for one person to capture the words, the emotions and the meaning when a lot of information is coming at them. This is where the team aspect comes in.

Like the tactical team, the negotiation team are also recruited for specific characteristics — one of which is patience. This team can play a long game like nobody's business. They can wait it out for hours, days or weeks — or, as in the case of the high-profile Waco, Texas, hostage situation in 1993, 51 days.

I mention earlier in this chapter that the success rate of a peaceful resolution in these situations is 95 per cent. It's encouraging, then, that this team with such a high success rate are using the exact same weapons we, too, are armed with — ears and a mouth.

In the business world, I've seen countless people enter into negotiations or sales conversations with high-stakes prospects like the *tactical* FBI team. They want to get in, get the job done quickly, and get out. They seem to believe you only get one chance to 'land the plane' in that meeting, and that's it.

As a result, the relationship is sacrificed and people play for *speed* of outcome, instead of *quality* of outcome.

I don't recall any sales commandment that suggests you only have one chance to convince someone to buy from you, but it seems that people treat the first meeting as the only meeting they will ever get. They bring out all their 'big guns' in terms of fancy presentations and dazzling testimonials.

Unfortunately, I've seen speed kill so many deals.

If, on the other hand, you choose to play more like the FBI negotiation team, you are more likely to be rewarded with quality outcomes. The process might seem slower, but the outcome will be more secure and the parties will enjoy a better relationship.

The work I do, and the process I teach, is unique. And I'm continually rewarded with the opportunity to connect with people who are interesting, influential and well known. In many of these situations, I take the opportunity to slow the conversation down, and be clear that I'm not there to pitch them anything.

I make it clear that I'd rather converse with them the right way, not the fast way, and that this first meeting is a chance to get to know each other a little and then see if it makes sense to have another meeting. I cannot recall one instance where one meeting hasn't resulted in further meetings.

Often a friend or colleague will hear I'm about to meet with a well-known person, and will then pressure me to go in with an 'ask' or a 'pitch'. But I always go in with the same objective, which I happily share with these people:

I'm not here to pitch you anything. I'm simply here so we can get to know each other a little, and then see if it makes sense to meet again after today.

Playing your sales and negotiation conversations like FBI negotiators is a smart strategy. Play the long game.

FAQ

Q: Julia, what's one thing that businesses need to do to succeed in sales?

A: There isn't just one thing they need to do. You need to do all the things.

Always use customer relationship management software

Customer relationship management software (otherwise known as a CRM) is cloud-based software you can use to record and store your interactions with prospects who come to you through marketing, inbound or outbound activity. It's an essential software investment that (when used correctly) gives you full visibility over your sales and revenue function, and helps you convert more opportunities.

If sales and revenue are important to you, you can't afford not to have a CRM.

Like most software, choosing the right CRM software can be a tricky field to navigate, and countless options are available. I've been exposed to CRMs for about 25 years and, even today, people still tell me about different CRM platforms that I've never heard of!

Even if you're not familiar with the term 'CRM', some of the following company and product names might be familiar to you: Salesforce, HubSpot, Zoho, Pipedrive, Microsoft Dynamics, Freshsales, Tall Emu, Bullhorn … there are too many to even name and new ones are popping up all the time.

Make sure you do your research, though. Many online software platforms *claim* to be a CRM, or have a CRM component, but they aren't. Let me explain with an analogy. A Swiss Army knife contains various tools, including a blade, a screwdriver and scissors. While it can be useful in some situations, each individual tool is not the best at any specific task when compared to specialised tools. The same concept applies when looking for a CRM.

Project management programs, productivity tools and enterprise resource planning (ERPs) might all be masquerading as CRMs but, I can tell you, they are not.

Don't be fooled into thinking you don't need a full CRM. In conversation with a prospective new client, I asked about their CRM and they proudly announced that they didn't need one, because their ERP was also a CRM. We had some conversation around this and I shared, from my professional experience, the risks involved in this belief. They were adamant no changes were required, so we both happily agreed to talk about this again if it became problematic.

The prospect became a client, and they soon learned the importance of aligning their CRM with a sales process, which their CRM (which wasn't a CRM) wasn't able to serve them with. It wasn't long before we were revisiting this conversation and they began implementing a proper, standalone CRM.

Here's the hierarchy for places to store your prospect and customer data, from the least beneficial to the most:

- *At the bottom of the list:* In your head.

- *A small step-up from that:* In your Outlook/calendar.

- *A decent step-up from that:* In an Excel spreadsheet (at least it's somewhere).

- *At the top of the list:* In your CRM (but you need to use it correctly).

As noted in the last point, having a CRM is still useless if you don't use it correctly. Ever heard the phrase 'rubbish in, rubbish out'? I have lost count of the number of companies who have asked me to review their CRM with the brief, 'We need a new one'. Whether they actually need a new one or don't, one aspect quickly becomes clear — they don't know how to use their current CRM properly.

Most business owners get excited about relentlessly checking their bank balance. Some people can lose time scrolling Instagram. I lose time trawling through the exciting data in my CRM! Yes, I admit, I'm weird — but hear me out!

Your CRM provides a world of stories, trends, possibilities and scenarios, which can help you accurately forecast and predict your business. It can tell you at the click of a button on a beautiful dashboard how much revenue should be hitting your bank account this week, this quarter, next quarter and next financial year. It can inform you of the time of the year when you can invest in seven more staff members and throw a bucketload of money into a marketing campaign. It can also tell you when you might need to let go of team members and tighten your belt. The positive part of that negative story is your CRM data will tell you this in advance, so it doesn't sneak up on you and, even better, you can put immediate plans in place to avoid this happening.

You can use the data from your CRM to drive exceptional coaching conversations with your team to motivate them and help them to reach great levels of self-achievement. This data can also highlight any opportunities that have been forgotten or are slipping through your fingers.

Here's a tip for new (and old) players, though: A CRM can open up a whole world of exciting and shiny new things. Don't be distracted by this, yet.

Many of these shiny things can stop you from even starting with a CRM, so for the purpose of teaching you The Infinite Sales System, I'm only going to comment on CRMs from a *sales process* perspective. Taking you down the track of all the fancy integrations, and all the marketing, automations and workflow options, would be a slippery slope and your project would be enormous — and expensive.

Start with the basics and follow the process outlined in the next part of this book. Avoid the temptation to build in all the fancy options right away because you won't use them, it will be very expensive and, even worse, your team won't use the CRM at all because you've made it too difficult and complicated for them.

Perfection is the enemy of progress, so just get started with a CRM and build the fancy stuff in later.

Keep it simple, just do the things.

FAQ

Q: Julia, which CRM do you use?

A: Knowing which CRM I use isn't helpful to you because my business is different from yours, and you will want to use a CRM differently from me. You might want to integrate your CRM with other software in your existing tech stack, for example, and you might want different bells and whistles on it than I do. Here's my professional advice, though, on which one to get: Just get one.

Also remember, missing the opportunities highlighted by your CRM can happen to the best of us — if you're not looking. I recently had a conversation with a client who confidently told me they were all over their CRM data. I asked them to run a specific report (which took them one minute) and I was able to identify $4.2 million in opportunities that had fallen between the cracks and they were about to lose.

Your CRM is the data house of your revenue machine.

If you already have a CRM in your business, it's crucial to not only have it aligned to your sales process, but also have a company culture around adoption and usage. If your team think it's great but either don't use it or only sometimes use it, it won't serve you.

As you make your way through this book, I will be highlighting how you should be using your CRM to support your success in applying The Infinite Sales System. In some of the early stages of the process, I outline CRM actions that relate to parts of the system you might not have learned, yet. These actions will become more evident as you progress through the system, but require a CRM action prior.

CHAPTER 4

GETTING READY FOR THE INFINITE SALES SYSTEM®

As already mentioned, I developed The Infinite Sales System for businesses that mostly operate in service or solution-based businesses. These businesses are writing contracts worth tens, hundreds of thousands or millions of dollars, which means they are developing relationships with their prospects and clients, and can experience a long buying cycle. Frequently, they don't associate themselves with being 'in sales'. People leading and working in these sorts of businesses are who I see as benefiting most from my system and this book — although if you're in sales and looking for a new way of doing things, you'll find loads of help here too.

The Infinite Sales System is a holistic system, providing you with a step-by-step and an end-to-end process to follow that's not based on tips and tricks. I outline the full process in the chapters in the next part. Underlying the methodology of the system, however, are some key principles and core approaches that keep the system running smoothly.

Without first explaining those principles, I wouldn't be setting you up for success when it comes to applying The Infinite Sales System.

And to put this in context, when I teach the system in person to clients, I spend seven hours (not in one hit, though!) on the underlying principles and approaches before we get into the actual system. If it wasn't necessary, we wouldn't do it.

I outline these essentials in this chapter — starting with the key principles.

Underlying principles of The Infinite Sales System

The following principles form the foundation for the whole of The Infinite Sales System. You need to get your head around these principles *before* you do anything else, *and* keep them in mind at every step of the process.

The 'trust-first' approach

What if I told you your ability to speak technically-brilliant, industry-related language can lead to you being less trustworthy. Would you believe me?

Some fascinating research into the science of making a first impression comes from psychologist Amy Cuddy, and I've adapted her findings into the sales arena.

Cuddy suggests that when we meet someone for the first time, we are immediately sizing up particular things about this person in order to figure out their character. We do this consciously and unconsciously.

What are some things that you size up in people when you meet them for the first time? Their style of language? Their personal grooming and appearance? Whether they are pleasant to talk to? Do they talk about themselves? Are they confident, arrogant or shy? What kind of shoes are they wearing?

We all can be a bit 'judgey-judgey' when meeting people, and one particular thing I size up in someone new is their handshake. Now, I'm not judging if they squeeze the hell out of my hand or if they give me the 'limp fish'. Instead, what I'm looking at is their eye contact and facial expression the moment our hands meet. Do they make eye contact and give me a warm smile and a friendly, genuine hello? Do they use my name? Or are they shaking my hand and looking at the floor or, even worse, looking past me at someone else they would rather talk to?

Cuddy suggests that what we are essentially trying to ascertain through all these first impression judgements is something quite simple: Can I trust this person, and are they competent?

Now, this first part to Cuddy's research, to be honest, seemed pretty common sense to me and not at all research-worthy. But where she took this research is where it gets interesting.

The research suggests that the order in which you obtain these two attributes — trust and competence — is 'make or break' for how the relationship progresses. If you make that first impression leading with competence, then trust is off the table — or, at least, much harder for you to gain.

 Spoiler alert: **In sales, building trust first is *far* more important than trying to impress someone with your technical brilliance.**

A common example of going in to a new conversation with someone and exhibiting a 'competence first' approach is where you drive the conversation and make it mainly about yourself. This kind of approach led to a phrase that I coined years ago — 'the show up and throw up' approach.

The 'show up and throw up' is when someone decides to vomit their greatness all over you, uninvited. It's possible you've done a show up and throw up over a new prospect, or maybe someone has done a show up and throw up all over you at a networking event! It's more common than you may think.

This approach doesn't always come from arrogance. Maybe the person is simply nervous or doesn't know what else to say, aside from talking about themselves. This doesn't make them a criminal by any means, but it can set up a negative impression from the start.

Let's imagine for a moment that you and I are at a business seminar for a day. There's a break in the schedule and I see you at the coffee machine. After we exchange our names, what's that one particular and infamous question that you're going to ask me next? Go on, you know it!

You're going to say, 'So, Julia, what do you do?'

Now, allow me to demonstrate what a 'competence-first' response looks like:

Well, I'm a sales strategist and a professional negotiator. I love what I do. In fact, I've worked for some of the biggest companies in the world, helping them to increase their sales and improve how they negotiate. I also provide a lot of media interviews on various business channels and I've won some awards for what I do. Here's where I went to university ... here are some of the companies I work with ... blah, blah, blah.

Now, just imagine that I was nervous and the 'show up and throw up' was simply a product of my nerves. Even so, what might you be thinking, as I vomit my greatness all over you, I wonder?

Stop talking!! or *Shut up*, or *I have to get away from this lady!*

In this example, my 'competence-first' approach is unlikely going to get you to trust me, because I've gotten you offside by how annoying I am!

Now, imagine we're still at that same seminar and we break for afternoon tea. I see you over at the doughnuts and I make a beeline for you, because, obviously, I think we're great friends now!

What are you thinking?! *Aaah! Here's she comes again!*

Let's say you quickly escape and end up talking to Morgan, and Morgan just happens to share with you she is having some very specific business challenges and she asks (coincidentally) if you might happen to know anyone who is a sales strategist or a professional negotiator. (I know, what are the chances?!)

Because you don't trust me, it's now possible you're going to do one of two things: you'll either reply that you don't know anyone in that field (even though we only met earlier) or you'll point me out and tell Morgan to definitely avoid talking to me. So you'll work against me because you don't trust me!

What a horrible outcome for me — and the only crime I may have committed was being really nervous and talking more than I should.

Yet, this competence-leading approach is very common in sales presentations. The seller takes up a lot of air time sharing why their company is market leading, how their services are first class and why their team are the most experienced.

But the research tells us that this turns people off. Worst yet, it can lead to you being seen as untrustworthy.

Now, let's turn the tables and talk about a trust-first approach.

Cuddy's research suggests that if you succeed in a trust-first approach, competency is automatically awarded to you — you don't even have to try!

This is the part of the research that really grabbed my attention. So I learned all about it, and then I overhauled my entire sales approach to be trust-first. When I started doing this well, I enjoyed some fast results.

First, my conversion ratio was continually increasing, and I was converting larger clients, faster than I ever had before. Second, something really interesting started happening ...

When I started my first session with a brand new client (not a prospect), at some point they would usually say something like, 'Julia, I realise I don't know much about you!' And yet, they had already engaged me.

What's fascinating about this is that no-one ever asks me where I went to school, what degrees I might have, which business awards I may have won, what media I have been featured in or who else I've worked with. People can google my credentials easily enough; however, no-one really cares about me verbally telling them about my accolades — instead, what I said and did, early on, made them trust me and feel like it was going to be okay to work with me.

A trust-first approach takes the pressure off you having to present cleverly crafted words about yourself, your team and your company.

A trust-first approach takes the pressure off you having to pitch or be extroverted, and it allows you to be more engaged in a collaborative conversation, more yourself and more calm. How enlightening.

How do you go about building that trust? Read on ...

FAQ

Q: So I'm at an event and someone asks me, 'What do you do?' How do I answer? Do I change the topic?

A: No! You give a short response, and then return serve with an open question that invites them to share about themselves. My response might go a bit like this (speaking slowly and calmly): 'I'm a sales strategist and professional negotiator, and my company helps businesses to implement a repeatable sales process. I'd love to ask, what's the reason you've come along to this event today?'

The trust equation

Consider someone you trust for a moment, and it can't be someone from your family or your partner. Now, keeping that person in mind, can you quantify exactly how you know you can trust them? Is it because they've never let you down? Because they have your back? Because you have history together?

Trust can be hard to quantify, but we do have a way to measure trust. This measurement is known as the *trust equation*, outlined by Harvard professors David Maister, Charles Green and Robert Galford in their book *The Trusted Advisor*, and shown in the following:

$$\text{TRUST} = \frac{\text{CREDIBILITY} + \text{RELIABILITY} + \text{INTIMACY}}{\text{SELF-ORIENTATION}}$$

Here's what each of the elements in the equation relate to:

- *Credibility:* Do you have the required skills, qualifications and the 'runs on the board'? If you're an engineer, for example, have you completed the relevant degree?

- *Reliability:* Can I depend on you, and what is your reputation like?

- *Intimacy:* What is your level of connection with people? (This element is an interesting one.)

- *Self-orientation:* What is your level of self-interest? This is the negative element in the equation. You could be the most credible and reliable person around, and people may feel some connection to you, but if they know you are just in it for yourself and are only interested in what's best for you, you're much less likely to be trusted.

All three elements on the top line of the equation are important; however, one carries more weight than the others. Which do you think it is? Take another look before I reveal the answer ...

It's intimacy. Again, all three attributes are important, but intimacy is a real needle-mover here.

Furthermore, intimacy is a spectrum. Down one end, we have 'connection' and, at the other end, we have what the FBI negotiators refer to as 'bonding'. (Not so) fun fact, this is where Stockholm syndrome occurs. (If you're not familiar with Stockholm syndrome, this occurs in a hostage/captor scenario where the hostage falls in love with the hostage taker.)

Great news: We're not going for anything up that end. ☺ We're going for a small step-up from connection, which is 'likeability'.

Likeability is formed through relatability — do we have kids the same age? Do we both love dogs but hate cats? Did we grow up in the same area? Are we both frustrated by the same industry challenges? Are we binging the same Netflix series?

Personal share: I do love a good show featuring Mexican or Columbian drug cartels! *Queen of the South, Ozark, Breaking Bad* are all favourites of mine. So, by chance, if we're chatting and I realise you also love those shows, we can talk for ages about them, and I give you more trust points because we have a strong bond over those shows.

To further the point about intimacy, it's so powerful that it can be used for good and for evil.

Using it for good is how start-ups get off the ground. They have no credibility or reliability (the other two elements above the line in the trust equation) because they only have an idea at this stage. But some investor seems to like the entrepreneur, they hit it off because they have connected, and they invest $2 million so they can get an office, hire a development team and start building out their idea.

I'd hazard a guess that if the opposite is the case and the entrepreneur is a jerk — no investment for them!

Where intimacy is used for evil is the space where con artists operate! Whenever you see people interviewed in the media after they've been scammed by some dodgy financial advisor, one thing you'll never hear them say is, 'We feel awful that we gave them $500 000 because, you know what? We never liked them, right from the start!'

No! They never say that! They are always surprised by how that person could have taken their money. They say things like, 'Our kids went to school together' or, 'We were friends for such a long time'.

The con artist *knows* what they are doing — they are using intimacy for evil.

More good news: We're not going for that end of the spectrum in our journey, either! We're going for the 'use it for good' space!

To really drive this point home, here are the two reasons this trust equation is so important:

1.   People buy from people they like.

2.   People are more likely to agree with people they like.

On that second point, consider someone you really don't like. When we feel this way about someone, we tend to go out of our way to disagree with them, and it's much easier to do so. On the other hand, if we genuinely have a lot in common with someone, we tend to go out of our way to agree with them.

This is how important trust and intimacy is.

Intimacy is the difference between lots of great prospects in your pipeline, and none.

Crucial questions

So, how do you achieve this intimacy and a trust-first process? You start by making your conversation less about yourself and more about someone else — and you do this by asking the right questions.

Asking high-quality questions will form the basis for many of the steps in The Infinite Sales System and, as you'll learn, the answers you get back are usually formed by the questions you ask, and the quality of those questions.

Ask a poor question, and you'll receive a poor answer or no answer at all. Ask a great question, and you'll be rewarded with a depth of insightful responses and riches of information you may not even expect.

You're likely already aware of open and closed questions.

Closed questions are those that grant you a 'yes' or 'no' answer. These questions start with the following:

- is

- are

- can

- do

- did

- does

- have

- has

- had

- will

- could

- should

- would.

They are questions like:

- Do you have a budget for this project?

- Have you worked with consultants in this field before?

- Is there a time frame you have in mind for this work?

- Are you familiar with our services?

These types of questions won't give you much information; however, the other, more significant, downside is they feel like you're trying to take something from someone. They create the impression you're only asking these questions so you can check a box, and then sell them something. They feel like data-collecting questions.

Open questions, on the other hand, are designed to reward you with lots of dialogue and plenty of collaborative conversation. They also allow your prospect to share what is important to them, in a safe space.

They start with:

- who

- what

- when

- where

- why

- how

- tell me (my favourite — the cheat's way of asking an open question).

However, even some questions that are open by default are actually terrible and won't give you much.

If you have children in your world, for example, and ask them, 'How was school today?', you generally get a response of 'good'. 'What did you learn today?' 'Nothing!'

Or, even on a Monday morning, what's the question we usually ask our colleagues? 'How was your weekend?' To which the response is usually, 'Good, thanks'. 'What did you get up to?' 'Oh, not much.'

So even though those questions are open by nature, they don't give us much. The skill is in asking high-quality open questions, so your prospect is given the space to share.

The following table (overleaf) provides some examples of how to shift closed questions to high-quality open questions.

Making the shift from closed to high-quality open questions

Closed question	Make the shift
Do you have a budget for this project?	Tell me about your budget for this project.
Are there milestones you're aiming for?	Tell me about the milestones along the way you want to reach.
Have you worked with consultants like us before?	What's been your experience working with consultants like us previously?
Are you familiar with our services?	Tell me what you've heard about our services.

It takes effort to naturally ask high-quality open questions and this is best practised all the time! Each time you engage with someone, try thinking up some good-quality open questions you can ask to get the conversation going. I like to challenge myself by seeing if I can ask a high-quality open question, and receive a long and detailed response. If I receive this, I know it's because of the quality of the question asked.

Once you become great at this, you'll find people will frequently comment on the questions you ask, and how insightful your questions are. Even more importantly, they will thoroughly enjoy talking with you, and you'll be enjoying great collaborative conversation and building a wonderful connection.

Changing how you ask questions will change your level of engagement. It will also give you more information about someone and gift you with reasons to find intimacy, so you connect. This matters, because (if you remember) people buy from people they like.

Once you've mastered high-quality open questions, you're ready for the next two types of questions.

Transactional and tactical questions

Knowing the difference between transactional and tactical questions will give you a competitive advantage because, when you can use them correctly, your prospect will likely be far more engaged with you, and they will find you to be far more insightful than any of your competitors.

Transactional questions are about the 'stuff and the things' — such as logistics, service choices, technical choices or delivery options. Much like closed questions, transactional questions also give the impression you're collecting data, or checking boxes, just so you can sell something to someone.

Tactical questions are about the situation, the bigger picture and what your prospect is ultimately trying to solve. They shift the conversation to be more collaborative, and they allow space for people to share what is most important to them.

If you lead your sales conversation with transactional questions, you risk being viewed (in Amy Cuddy's eyes) as going in competence-first, which, as covered earlier in this chapter, means it is harder to become trusted. In addition, by leading with these questions, you appear no different from your competitors, so you give your prospect no reason to see you as better, more professional or superior.

Pro tip: Mastering tactical questions can also reduce the likelihood of being challenged on your price down the track.

By leveraging tactical questions instead, you take the time to ask insightful questions, which often have your prospect thinking, or even telling you something like, 'No-one has ever asked us these questions before'. And what a great sign that is when it happens.

Imagine a conversation with a new prospect when you lead with questions such as the following:

- What kind of services are you after?

- How much are you looking to spend?

- When are you looking for this to be completed?

- Who do you want to be involved in this?

- What kind of materials do you want us to quote for you?

These transactional questions are open questions, but they create the impression you're just collecting information so you can present a proposal or a quote.

Now imagine serving the same prospect these questions:

- Tell me about your business in relation to these services?

- How is your customer impacted when this works well?

- What challenges are you currently experiencing with these services?

- What is the difference between a good and a great provider?

- How will you know you've selected the right provider for this project?

- If we were to work together, how could we be easy for you to partner with?

Can you see and feel the difference?

The first (transactional) questions can be received as check-box questions so you can put a proposal together.

The second (tactical) questions are more likely received as you genuinely caring about helping someone to solve a problem.

FAQ

Q: But Julia, we need to ask those transactional questions so we know what the prospect wants. How else do we learn that information to put a proposal together?

A: You're right. These questions are essential to ask—just not at the beginning of your conversation, where your focus should be on building connection. Later on in our process, I show you when to ask those more detailed questions.

Strategic silence

Even after you've mastered what kinds of questions to ask, you need to keep one very important warning in mind: your questions can be completely undone if you're not skilled at knowing *how* to ask the question, and then waiting patiently for the answer.

One habit I notice in many people during sales conversations is that they aren't comfortable to ride out the silence during any pauses.

This silence makes them feel awkward, so they fill it with something, anything, and doing so has the potential to undo any trust or professionalism that has been built so far.

Continually filling that silence can also mean you're perceived as panicked and frantic. Now, who loves to do business with anyone who's panicked? No-one, that's who!

The opposite of panic is calm. So, by injecting strategic silence into your conversation, you're also injecting calm. People love calm people.

Being perceived as calm also significantly increases your level of professionalism, because it demonstrates a high level of self-control and self-awareness.

If you're reading this and thinking you know that silence, and you do feel awkward and panicked in it, I have great news for you. I've conducted a research project on all the deaths that have ever occurred in the history of the world, and I've concluded that not one person has ever died from 'awkward silence'. So I can confidently tell you, you're going to be fine. ☺

Joking aside, I know 'sitting in the silence' sounds simple, but can be really hard. By nature, I can talk to a tree, but if I bring that characteristic into a sales conversation, I risk being too dominating and not listening, which will turn people off. Silence is a learned skill, and something many people are not great at, simply because they are not practising it.

The practice here is to have the skill to ask the right question, and then shut up. Say nothing and just wait.

Realistically, if you ask a great question, and your prospect isn't saying anything, what are they doing? They're thinking! So if you were to cut this off and jump in, give them options or repeat the question, you will have undone the power of your great question.

Another enemy here (in general conversations as well as in sales conversations) is something called 'prompting', which can also have an extremely negative impact. Prompting is mostly a nervous habit where someone asking a question isn't comfortable to let the silence ride out, so they prompt the conversation along, thinking they are helping the other person out.

This hit me (metaphorically) smack in the face about 14 years ago when I was single and on the dating scene.

I had a date with someone who, I need to point out, was a lovely person. They just weren't right for me. But their conversation during the date made me realise this habit of prompting, and now I see it show up in sales conversations, or really any conversation.

This person, let's call them 'The Prompter', would engage me in conversation using questions something like the following:

So, Julia, you say you're not from Perth originally, what brought you here? Was it your work, or maybe you came for a holiday or you'd just heard Perth was a great place, what's the reason you moved here?

And then ...

What kinds of things do you like to get up to in your spare time? Do you like the beach, or maybe you enjoy sports or exploring or maybe quiet time to yourself, what do you like to do?

And then ...

What is it you do for work? Do you work for a large company based in the office, or do you work for yourself, what field of work are you in?

You can imagine how frustrating this was! I would barely get a word in, and I felt like The Prompter was putting words in my mouth. Their approach made me want to disengage, which is why I only had one date with this person!

Here's the formula prompters follow:

Ask a high-quality open question → make it multiple choice → paraphrase the question.

Even worse, prompting is usually done in the one sentence, with the questioner barely taking a breath!

Imagine you are trying to have a conversation with someone in a calm and quiet, one-on-one setting, but behind them fireworks are going off, then balloons and streamers come from the ceiling, and a marching band appears and is going forward and back in front of you both. You don't know where to look!

This is the same response we get when prompting.

You'll notice, the conversation starts off strong, with a great question, but then goes downhill pretty quickly! Here's how this shows up in sales conversations:

Tell me about your experience working with engineers on this project, have you had a good experience before or maybe you're looking to change things and do something different with this project, can you share with me what you've tried before?

Or:

Tell me about the budget you're allocating to this project, is this something you have set ideas about and you've got a figure in mind already or maybe you're unsure at this stage, can you tell me about what you're looking to invest in this work?

Or:

> *How did you come to learn about us, is it because you've heard of us through industry contacts or maybe you've seen the work we've done on X project, I wonder how did you hear about us?*

Again, prompting is asking an open question, making it multiple choice, and then paraphrasing the question. And, in case it wasn't obvious, prompting is bad.

Imagine instead having the same conversation, but starting it by asking, 'Tell me about your experience working with engineers so far'. And then waiting calmly for a response. Or asking, 'What kind of budget have you come up with for this project?' Or, 'How did you come to hear about us?'

This is a much 'cleaner' way to converse with your prospect.

Prompting your prospect is a sure-fire way to kill the conversation, limit your engagement and make you annoying and confusing.

 # A confused mind always says 'no'.

'No' can mean your prospect won't buy from you. 'No' can also mean they move to a place of indecision. Just like a restaurant menu with 25 main meals to choose from, offering multiple options while prompting becomes confusing and makes decision-making more difficult.

Applying strategic silence in your sales conversations (and everyday conversations) will reward you with much more collaborative conversations, and you'll find people are much more willing to speak with you and share important information. And as a further bonus, mastering this will help you to become easier to buy from.

This is one technique that's a game changer. Try it the next time you put this book down and are speaking to someone, you won't be sorry. (To hear this strategy in action, check out my 'How to use strategic silence' episode of the *Negotiate Anything* podcast, available via Spotify or a quick online search.)

Ask your question, and shut up.

FAQ

Q: But what if they didn't hear my question? Aren't I being helpful by making it easier for them to answer?

A: If they didn't hear you, they will ask you to repeat your question. You're not making it easier for them—you're leading the conversation and risking them feeling like you're manipulating them into giving you the answer you want to hear.

Muscle memory

As I mention in chapter 3, as a youngster I was a gymnast, and I loved the sport. However, it was, and still is, quite a dangerous sport because with one wrong move you risk catastrophic injury.

Much like any sport or activity that someone is hoping to become great at, the fundamentals of gymnastics must be mastered before the more difficult skills can be tried.

Mastering these fundamentals, and I mean true mastery, takes exorbitant amounts of practice and effort. It takes thousands of repetitions of the most basic (and, often, the most boring) skills.

As I also cover in chapter 3, one reason repetitious practice is necessary is because it builds muscle memory. In the world of gymnastics, athletes are taught how to fall safely, and they practise this again and again. So if something goes wrong, muscle memory kicks in, and they fall safely without incurring injury.

This building of muscle memory is no different when you're learning to master sales and negotiation skills.

When put in high-stress or high-stakes situations (such as sales conversations), humans are wired to react, defend and justify, which are impulsive responses. Stress responses also kick in — fight, flight or freeze.

By practising the skills and techniques featured in The Infinite Sales System, you'll be building muscle memory. So when you're in a sales conversation, you'll have the right response, at the right time, delivered in the right way.

Imagine you are explaining your services to a high-stakes prospect and you present your price. They respond by telling you that price is too expensive and much more than they had expected.

Without muscle memory, you might do any number of things — for example, you may start to justify your price and outline all the reasons you are priced as such. Or you might freeze and not know what to say, or immediately offer a discount, which sees you lose credibility.

With the right muscle memory during this scenario, you'll respond the right way to the price challenge, and will be able to continue your conversation in a purposeful way that will result in winning an opportunity at full price, with a happy client.

Muscle memory can be built in the key skills and techniques in this program, but only through *continuous repetition* of these skills and techniques. You can practise these purposefully in a repetitious way with a colleague, friend or family member, no differently to how you might ask them to hit a few tennis balls back and forward with you if you wanted to improve your tennis game. For example, you might ask them to listen to you reel off rounds of open questions about a particular topic.

The following table outlines the key skills you should build muscle memory in, and some daily instances where you can practice. (Some of these skills have already been discussed; others are covered in later chapters.)

Key skills and techniques to build muscle memory in

Skill or technique	Building muscle memory
Open questions	• Ask them anytime you're talking with someone.
	• Use them to get your kids or partner to share more after school or work.
	• Practise them with your colleagues at the start of a meeting — three minutes of open questions.
	• When someone disagrees with you, ask an open question.
Strategic silence	• Use after you've asked a question.
	• In every conversation you have, try to pause before you respond.
Summary statements	• Use these every time you talk to someone — your colleagues, kids, friends or Uber driver!
Objection handling	• Whenever someone disagrees, objects or rejects you, recognise it, and pause before responding. Then ask them to share more with you.

I would go as far as suggesting that any time you interact with another human, you can find an opportunity to practise some, if not all, of the skills and techniques in this book.

 There is *always* a chance to ask a better question, pause before you answer, respond not react, or summarise what was implied.

The more frequently you practice these skills in low-stakes situations, the more success you will enjoy when the stakes are high.

Core approaches of The Infinite Sales System

Now that you have a better idea of the underlying principles of The Infinite Sales System, let me outline its core approaches. These aspects also run through every step of the process.

The three core approaches are:

- *Qualify:* This is about helping you get in front of more qualified opportunities, rather than just any opportunity. You can start to learn pretty quickly, even before you've met with a prospect, if meeting with them is going to be a good investment of your time and theirs. You do this by qualifying them.

- *Convert:* This covers the 'what to say, when to say it and what to do' aspects of conducting that first meeting with a prospect, which I call a 'first sales meeting' (see chapter 6). This approach also teaches you how to start winning the business from the first conversation, how to charge full price (or more) and have clients thrilled to pay it, how to shorten the buying time, how to nail your value proposition and how to stand out in a competitive industry.

- *Follow up:* This is all about doing what it says on the tin, following up — which is exactly what to do, after you have sent your proposal. This is where you also play the long game with prospects who aren't ready to buy from you immediately. As you will learn during chapter 9, follow up is strategic and relentless.

This isn't my first rodeo, so I've seen it all in terms of sales experiences. One common situation is that someone has a 'big' opportunity and so they put lots of effort into their sales presentation. The prospect then invites them to send a proposal, which they do. And then, they wait.

Let me tell you, 'waiting' is a terrible business strategy. So is 'luck', and so is 'hope'. I hear professionals say things like, 'I've sent the proposal, I hope we win it!' Or they tell each other 'good luck' when they are on the way to meet a good prospect.

Studies have shown that more than 80 per cent of new business is converted after the proposal is sent. And that it takes between 5 and 12 value-added follow-up phone calls before it converts. So in simple terms, this means that most of your new clients will convert during the follow up phase of your sales process. Yet, only 44 per cent of people follow up more than once!

With these key principles and core approaches in mind, let's get into the nitty-gritty of The Infinite Sales System.

PART II

THE INFINITE SALES SYSTEM®

Now you have the fundamental principles and approaches on board, this part is all about showing how to embed those skills and techniques as you progress through The Infinite Sales System.

The system consists of five steps:

- *Step one: Qualification:* How to determine if your prospect is the right type of opportunity for you to meet with.

- *Step two: First sales meeting:* A step-by-step guide for conducting your first meeting with a prospect.

- *Step three: Meeting follow up:* What to do after your first meeting, so the process continues moving forward.

- *Step four: Second sales meeting:* How to shorten the decision-making time and learn about any reservations your prospect has, so you can address them.

- *Step five: Follow up:* What to do if your prospect decides not to buy from you immediately and how to play the long game without being annoying.

This process is repeatable and trackable. And here's the great news: the more competitive the industry you work in, the more effective this process can be for you.

So, strap yourselves in. Let's begin!

CHAPTER 5

STEP ONE: QUALIFICATION PROCESS

Your sales process really starts here when you have a human to interact with. Either someone has 'inbounded' you, which means they have contacted you first through your website, a phone call or even a referral, or you have someone you've gone 'outbound' to, and they have also agreed to meet with you.

Before this meeting occurs, you want to ensure this person is a *qualified* prospect, so you can respect both your time and theirs. And you start working that out by looking at their motivation *and* capability.

Combining motivation with capability

Imagine you were talking to a prospect and they were highly motivated to partner with you. What would they be saying or doing to give you that indication? They would likely be asking detailed questions, showing enthusiasm in the conversation, asking about pricing, time lines and delivery, and sharing more about their organisation and pain points. You can probably work out if someone is keen, or motivated, to partner with you. It's usually not that difficult. But this isn't enough. You also need that person to be *capable* of partnering with you.

 For someone to be capable of buying from you, you need them to be the decision-maker, and have the appropriate budget and time line requirements.

This brings us to the motivation and capability scale (shown in the following figure).

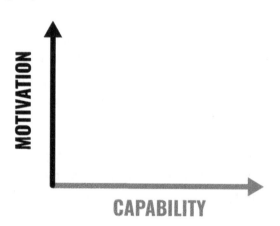

The motivation and capability scale allows you to take a step back and work out how qualified your prospect is.

Let me give you an example. Imagine I were a car enthusiast (of which the opposite is actually the case). If I were, I'm sure I would love to drive a Porsche Cayenne SUV. If I went to the Porsche dealership,

I would have done my prior research and I'd have some great questions to ask. I'd ask about features, accessories and other additions. I would be extremely motivated to buy this car — the most motivated, in fact!

But one big deal-breaker would likely suggest I'm not actually *capable* to make this purchase, based on the motivation and capability scale. I may not have up to 300 'Gs' to drop on a fancy car like this! So, in this case, I'm highly motivated, but low on capability.

I refer to these types of situations as having 'happy ears'.

Happy ears occur when we hear all the right sounds, and we ignore all the data that might tell us a different story. Having happy ears is very common in sales conversations. I hear lots of people sharing great stories, with so much enthusiasm about prospects they've met with. Often when I dig a little, however, we find out they are talking to someone who isn't a decision-maker, or a company who will not have the budget required for the project.

That's high motivation, low capability (shown in the following figure).

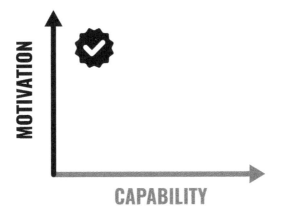

On the flip side, it's also not great to be speaking with a prospect who is highly capable, but low on motivation (shown in the following figure). Say you want to have a conversation with a huge prospect, who you know has the budget to afford your services, but this person has no urgency to partner with you, so in this instance, it's a non-starting conversation.

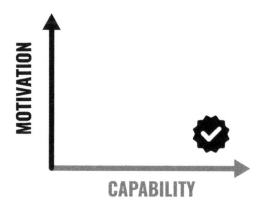

You need to be aiming to meet with people who are *both* high in motivation and high in capability.

This (shown in the following figure) helps you avoid the trap of happy ears, and allows you to truly assess where the prospect might be on that scale and if they are even worth pursuing.

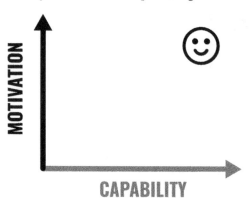

Finding a sales qualified lead

I'm going to hit you with some jargon and acronyms now. At the very start of the sales process, people are called marketing qualified leads, or MQLs. An MQL can be someone you know very little about in terms of the problem they want to solve, their urgency or even if you can help them. They are, in effect, a human with a pulse.

By asking this prospect a series of short questions, you can start to learn if they are a sales qualified lead, or an SQL. An SQL is someone you know a few things about — at least enough so you think, *This sounds like a great opportunity — we've got a live one here!*

To uncover your SQL, you need to create some qualification questions for them to answer, prior to you meeting with them. Your qualification questions can be embedded in your website on your 'contact us' form, sent out in a survey (which is what I do), or asked over the phone if someone calls you directly.

Pro tip: You should approach these questions, and how they are answered, as if you have plenty of business on, and you are *ruling people out* who you do not wish to work with, for whatever reason.

If your qualification questions aren't tailored enough, you'll end up meeting too many people and wasting both their time and yours, conversion ratios will be lower, you'll be working with the wrong types of clients, and you'll be less productive and less engaged in your role. Is that a convincing enough reason?

Here are some examples of qualification questions:

1. What's the reason you'd like us to get in touch with you?

2. What services might you be interested in from the following?
    a. Z
    b. Y
    c. X
    d. W
    e. V

3. How many employees does your organisation have?
    a. <50
    b. 51–250
    c. 251–1000
    d. 1001 +

4. Tell us about the budget you're allocating for this project.
    a. Unsure at this stage
    b. <$50 000
    c. $50 000–$150 000
    d. $150 000–$250 000
    e. $250 000 +

5. Tell us about the timing for this enquiry.
    a. This is the single most important priority we have right now.
    b. We know we need a solution and are looking to implement in three to six months.
    c. We're just gathering information at this stage.

6. Tell us about your role in the company.

   a. I am the key decision-maker on this project.

   b. I am tasked with collecting information on this project.

7. What else would you like to share with us?

8. How did you find out about us?

It's important to ask questions that guide your prospect to the kind of work you want to attract.

For example, if you only work with large 'tier 1' organisations, and the question 3 options in the preceding list only go up to a total range of 20–100 employees, you are going to give the impression you only work with smaller businesses.

You also want to be sure to ask question 6, so you know if you're dealing with the decision-maker. (If you're not at this stage, you'll want to make sure you will be by your first meeting.)

In my business, I do not attend the meeting if this survey isn't completed. If the survey has not been completed the day before the meeting, the prospect is contacted with a friendly reminder and offered an opportunity to reschedule, which then sees them complete my survey.

This non-negotiable of having to complete the survey before the meeting shocks many people. They fear it will cause too many prospects to cancel their appointment. But it's crucial to value your time. Also, if your prospect isn't prepared to invest one minute to complete your survey, how prepared are they to invest time and resources into your services?

This survey also 'warms them up', and lets them know your meeting is important and not just a simple catch up. The process is also more likely to solidify your meeting because they have already invested time in the preparation.

The proof is in the pudding — I have 100 per cent show rates to my first sales meetings.

As always, keep it simple here — you're not trying to learn everything about them with the survey. You're just trying to learn if they are an MQL or an SQL. MQLs stay in your CRM for marketing purposes for future contact. If they are an SQL, they progress and are booked for a first sales meeting, which you set up and send the calendar invitation for. (I dive into first sales meetings in the next chapter.)

FAQ

Q: But if I use that budget question and people are scared off, don't we lose the opportunity?

A: Not at all. In fact, you've saved yourself time (and respected their time) because if they, say, only had a budget of $25 000, then you would know right away they are a small company, or aren't willing to invest in a proper solution.

Q: What do I tell them if I learn they are an MQL?

A: You politely thank them for providing you with information about their enquiry and then respectfully let them know you are not best-placed to serve them. Then, you can offer to make a warm introduction to another provider who you trust.

CRM usage

Once your qualification questions have been answered and you've determined a prospect *is* an SQL, you need to enter their details into your CRM and ensure some early tasks are completed.

The following table outlines the steps you need to take at this stage. (Note that some of these tasks will be discussed in more detail in the next chapter.)

Setting up an SQL in your CRM

CRM field	Title/subject	Notes
Account	As applicable	Enter the company (account) name
Contact	As applicable	Enter full contact details of each person you're in contact with at the company
Task	Qualification survey	Enter date survey was sent/ completed; then, mark task as complete
Meeting	First sales meeting	Schedule for the day of your first sales meeting
Task	Send Loom video	Schedule for the day of your first sales meeting
Task	Send proposal	Schedule for the day after your first sales meeting

CHAPTER 6

STEP TWO: THE FIRST SALES MEETING

This chapter's a biggie — and for good reason. So grab your beverage of choice, your highlighter and post-it-notes, and get ready for the most impactful part of the system!

This is the chapter you'll want to read several times, and that's for a few reasons. First, there are many individual components to learn. Second, this is like learning a new language — you can't just listen to one lesson, you need to review and practice the language repeatedly. And third, this has the biggest impact on whether your prospect views you as a 'nice to have', or a 'must-have'.

While other important steps come after this one, your first sales meeting is critical in building your relationship with your prospect, finding out more about their needs and making tailored recommendations based on these needs.

This chapter takes you through all these components of your first sales meeting and more, with lots of tips and insights along the way. But first, let's start with the basics ...

Basics of first sales meetings

The basics I've included here are non-negotiable. They also may seem a little obvious, but I've seen so many people get them wrong — and lose prospects. So treat them as gospel. Further to this, if you want to increase your conversion ratio and have the ability to increase your prices, then the first meeting steps aren't simply 'tips and tricks' to add in or adapt as you see fit. They are to be conducted as the process recommends.

First sales meetings are always conducted either face to face, *or* over a Zoom or Teams call. They are *never* conducted over the phone, and absolutely *never* conducted over email exchanges or over a meal.

First sales meetings should always be scheduled for one hour — not 30 minutes, not 45 minutes, and most definitely not a 'let's have a quick chat about how we could help'. They are one hour.

Whenever I reference this next sentence, I feel a bit like I'm quoting a Dr Seuss book, but here's a little rhyme to remember:

We meet face to face or on a screen.

Not by phone, nor email thread.

Not in cafes, where lunches are spread.

Another phrase I joke about is 'have a meal, lose a deal'. Here's why.

The first sales meeting is designed to be as much as an experience for your prospect, as it is a safe space for them to share what's important to them. You can't do what you need to do in that meeting over lunch. There will be waiters, food, eating and interruptions — as well as the risk of random people who either of you may know, who stop by to say hello and, heaven forbid, are invited to join you!

I once had a promising first sales meeting booked with a prospect and they told me they would love to take me to lunch for the meeting and that we could talk there. Anyone who knows me knows how much I love food, so an offer of lunch will always get my attention, but not if it intends to be combined with a first sales meeting. I politely said no to lunch and instead let them know I'd prefer a quiet meeting room where I could focus on them.

A first sales meeting, ideally, takes place in a quiet meeting space. I'll occasionally agree to meet at a café, but I'll then add in some extra precautions. I'll ensure we are in a quiet space, and I'll get there early and message them to ask for their coffee order so we are uninterrupted during the meeting and I can get into the zone.

Remember — you need one full hour for a first sales meeting, not 30 minutes, and not 45 minutes. This is a process designed to fill an hour, and you need that person's full attention for that time.

FAQ

Q: What if they only offer me 30 minutes?

A: A first sales meeting cannot be successfully completed in 30 minutes. You need one full hour. If a prospect tells me they can only spare 30 minutes, I respectfully share something like the following:

> *Thanks for wanting to meet with me, and I'm looking forward to it. May I respectfully let you know that I won't be able to do our conversation justice in 30 minutes, so I can't make that time. It sounds like this conversation is an important one to you, though, so I'd prefer to do this the right way, not the fast way. Would you be against finding another time when you do have an hour?*

In every instance I've had this occur, I end up getting an hour. I find this is because I'm demonstrating up-front that I'm going to bring them value.

Components of first sales meetings

A first sales meeting has several components, so let me break them down for you one by one. At the end of this chapter, I also show you how to put all these components together, so your meeting flows smoothly.

The components of the first sales meeting are shown in the following figure.

CHITCHAT
Share something personal

4-STEP AGENDA
Meeting agenda

OPEN QUESTIONS
All about them

SUMMARY
What you've heard

I CAN HELP YOU
Hero statement

EMOTIONAL BENEFITS
What problems do you solve for them?

RECOMMENDATIONS
It's your turn — all about you

NEXT STEPS
Closing the meeting off

Do the chitchat

At the start of the meeting the first most logical thing to happen is some rapport building. I'm always asked, 'Julia, do I get straight down to business? Do I do the chitchat, or do I not do the chitchat?'

Do the chitchat!

The chitchat should only go for five to seven minutes, and you should come prepared to share something personal of yourself. I'm not talking about sharing your deepest darkest secrets, but something safe and informal. Here are some ideas:

- what your kids got up to over the weekend

- a win you've had for the week

- something that's hijacked your week

- something you're looking forward to.

These give people reasons to find commonalities with you. Do you recall (from chapter 4) why this is so important? It's because people buy from people they like, and people are more inclined to agree with people they like.

These five to seven minutes of informal rapport building allow you both to find things you have in common, which sets the tone for the meeting that you are someone to be trusted.

FAQ

Q: How much personal information should I share?

A: Only what you are comfortable with. When meeting someone brand new, providing some easy, informal and safe topics to allow them to connect with you on, is often helpful. An easy one to start with is a simple question like, 'How's your week/morning going so far?' It's likely they will answer with something very non-descriptive like, 'Pretty good, thanks. How about you?' How you answer this can make a huge difference to the connection you build.

When they 'return serve' with this question, I never reply with the standard, 'Good, thank you'. I'm always prepared with a safe and informal response that gives them an opportunity to step in and connect with me. I might tell them that I've had a tough morning getting the kids off to school. I might share that I had an exciting win yesterday (and I would tell them about this win). Or it could be something interesting I did on the weekend. By sharing something personal, you help make the conversation more collaborative.

Outline your 4-step agenda

Either you think time is getting on (don't look at your watch!) or the chitchat is running thin, so you can now steer the conversation by transitioning into the business side of things.

The 4-step agenda is your key to setting up for first sales meeting success. It puts you in the driver's seat, and allows you to steer the meeting in a collaborative way (and not a dominating way). And, as with any good meeting, providing an agenda is a respectful way of letting them know what you'll cover in your conversation.

The following is a run-through of the 4-step agenda, and it starts with a subtle phrase that you can throw in as soon as you feel ready to steer away from the chitchat:

Well, Vishnu, I want to respect your time today, so shall we get started?

1. *I've come prepared to ask you some questions to learn about the current situation and what you're looking to achieve.*

2. *Based on what you share, I'll be able to make some recommendations or even give you some advice.*

3. *Then, we can agree what the next steps might be.*

4. *Does that sound okay to you?*

Note that I've added the numbers in this example for your reference. You don't need to number each item off with your prospect.

In my experience and after having used this hundreds of times, and my clients using it thousands of times, what tends to happen now is that your prospect responds with a 'yes', and they pause and wait for you to begin.

In real time, this 4-step agenda takes about 17 seconds. You should stick to this time (give or take a few seconds!) and avoid building it out.

When I've seen it used terribly, it goes something like this:

Thanks, Vishnu. I want to respect your time, so shall we get started?

Well, I've come prepared to ask you some questions today so I can learn about your company and what you're looking to achieve. So

I'll cover things like your current challenges and how you think we could help you and which people will be involved in this project in your company as well as your time line and budget for this work and how important this project is.

Then, when I've got all that information, I'll be able to make some recommendations or give you some advice and I'll also tell you all about our services, products and people, and I'll take you through our company history and the reasons why we can help you. I'll also share our pricing structure and how we like to partner with people just like you and even some case studies so I can show you some of the work we've done in this space.

Then, we'll talk about what the next steps are from here, which will be about sending you a proposal and setting up another meeting for us to talk again.

Have you fallen asleep, yet?

You can see the issues here, right? Avoid building the agenda out. Stick to the succinct version provided first, and learn it by heart. In its current form it's succinct, and it works.

Here it is again:

Well, Vishnu, I want to respect your time today, so shall we get started?

I've come prepared to ask you some questions to learn about the current situation and what you're looking to achieve. Based on what you share, I'll be able to make some recommendations or even give you some advice. Then, we can agree what the next steps might be. Does that sound okay to you?

This also gives you an elevated level of professionalism because, by nature, people like to be led, so you taking charge gives them comfort that you know what you're doing.

Just do the things.

Then, simply ask permission to take notes, and off you go.

FAQ

Q: What if they hijack me and just want to know about what we do, and they don't want to answer my questions?

A: Let them know that you came prepared this way because you thought it was the best way to respect them. You will most definitely be telling them all about your company later in the conversation, but you wanted to respect them and ask about them first.

Q: Can I take notes on my laptop or iPad?

A: Ideally, no. A screen is an unnecessary barrier between you, and especially if you're in an online meeting, taking digital notes will see them disengage.

Use open questions

The following comment was made to me during a first sales meeting with prospects at a training organisation, who have since become valued clients:

Julia, I've been timing you and you've barely said anything for 40 minutes. We've pretty much talked the whole time.

This is what I'm hoping for! You want your prospects to talk more, and (as covered in chapter 4), you facilitate this through high-level open questions.

Your open questions are the most important part of your first sales meeting and are crucial to you doing well. They allow you to learn everything important to your prospect about their business, their feelings, and their challenges and successes. Taking them through your questions is also designed to be an experience for them, where they are genuinely reflecting on their answers. If done correctly, they will likely comment on your insightful questions.

In my 26 years' experience in sales, I've seen enough sales interactions to know that it takes a level of mastery to do this part of the sales process well. Most people in sales conversations tend to fast-forward this part because they either:

- get too excited about telling prospects how they can help

- make assumptions about the challenges.

In relation to the first point, be calm. Don't get excited. By all means be engaged and enthusiastic, but being too excited can also turn people away.

In relation to the second point, I know that you know how to help them. To some degree, they also know that you know how to help them, which is why they agreed to meet with you in the first place.

The first sales meeting isn't about you impressing them with how much you know, or how quickly you can show them that you know. Your questions are designed to take them on a journey of the situation, which can't be fast-forwarded.

In chapter 4, I shared the importance of being purposeful and deliberate with your words and using high-level open questions, so you don't confuse people and you keep their engagement. As a further example of this, say you were a digital marketing agency meeting with a prospect. Let me show the difference between a purposeful open question and a poor one. Can you tell which question is the great one?

- So, can you tell me about your business?

- So, can you tell me about your business in relation to your digital marketing strategy?

Remember, you only have one hour for a first sales meeting, so asking the first question could see you losing 10 to 15 minutes on the answer to that question alone and, worst still, learning nothing about what you really want to know.

Asking the second, more targeted question allows your prospect to get straight to the heart of the matter, and share all about what you need to hear to help them.

Let me flesh this idea out with a family example. My uncle was a GP, and my aunt once told me about the time he learned the power of purposeful questions. When the stereotypical old ladies came in for appointments, he used to ask them, 'So, Mavis, how have you been?' And then Mavis would share all about her grandchildren, her latest gardening project and how her card-playing friends were. Before he knew it, 10 minutes had passed in what was a 15 minute booking.

He then changed and kicked off every appointment with, 'So, Mavis, what's the reason you've come to see me today?' This allowed him to get to the heart of the matter, and helped ensure he had maximum time to discuss and explore the challenge at hand in a focused way.

Your questions should serve you in the same way.

When I'm in a first sales meeting, I never say, 'So, tell me about your business.' Instead, I always kick off with, 'So, tell me about your business in relation to sales.' My prospects always then jump straight into telling me valuable information about this topic.

Have a list of 15 to 20 follow-up questions, and this list should be exactly the same for every first sales meeting.

Part of the value of The Infinite Sales System is that it's repeatable. If your questions are constantly changing, then measuring and tracking progress becomes impossible.

Your questions should be designed to take your prospect on a guided path through the following stages:

- What is the current situation in relation to the reason you're meeting (that is, your services)?

- What is working well, or has been working well?

- What are the challenges, frustrations and related impact on the business?

- What does success look like?

- How might you work together successfully?

When my team work directly with clients on implementing The Infinite Sales System in a business, part of our process is to produce for them a customised formal standard operating procedure (SOP) document for continual reference.

Much like you might show a new employee a procedural document for how to get their IT set up, this SOP document becomes the reference guide for how that business converts new opportunities.

Something my clients continue to find fascinating is how transferable the questions I recommend are across industries and sectors. Many clients tell me how unique they are; however, it usually turns out that most of the questions I produce for my clients in their SOP document are largely the same. This gives them a high degree of confidence, because it means the sales process is truly repeatable and doesn't need to change every time.

I've provided a list of possible questions here. For the purpose of this exercise, I've tailored the questions to employees of a digital marketing agency who are meeting with a prospective client. (Of course, they already know this prospect is an SQL, because they have sent the qualification questions from the previous chapter.) While you will certainly need questions specifically related to nuances in your industry, you should still be able to apply most of the following questions to your products or services:

- Can you tell me about your business in relation to your digital marketing strategy?

- What are all the things currently going well with this?

- Can you tell me about some of the most impactful digital marketing you've conducted?

- What are the things you'd like your customers to say about you?

- What frustrations or challenges are you experiencing with your digital marketing?

- How long have you been experiencing this?

- What have you tried so far to address this?

- Why is now the right time for a conversation about this?

- What is the impact of getting this right?

- What is the impact of changing nothing and continuing on as you are?

- How could we be easy for you to partner with?

- What would a successful partnership between us look like?

- How would we measure our success if we worked together?

- What do you see as the difference between a good digital marketing agency and a great one?

- What are your decision-making criteria for working with new providers?

- What barriers might we run into that would stop our conversation moving forward?

- Which elements in a partnership do you value, aside from price?

- Why might we be the right people to help you?

- If you happened to believe we are the right people to help you, what are the next steps, from your end, after our conversation today?

- What else haven't I asked you?

In my company, I currently do all the sales, and this is for three reasons:

1. I love the sales process and taking prospects through the experience.

2. I keep my own skills sharp through this continual practice.

3. My conversion ratio is continually between 79 and 84 per cent.

Because I've conducted so many first sales meetings, I have narrowed my list of questions down to nine.

I ask these exact same nine questions of everyone. It takes me about 40 minutes to get through them.

As you begin this process, you should take your total list of questions to all your first sales meetings, because it will prompt you on what to ask and in what order. Don't feel you need to cut your list down to nine questions like I have, because it will take you quite some time to work out which questions provide the most valuable answers for you and so get to your default list of questions.

Remember — *how* you ask questions is just as important as *what* you're asking.

Just because you have a list, it doesn't mean you're interrogating people. As your prospects answer each question, you may add a few 'filler' questions in — such as, 'Can you tell me more about that?' or, 'What do you mean by that?'

Getting through the questions and still coming across as conversational and collaborative rather than robotic also takes practice. Grab a colleague or a friend and practise on them. It might feel strange, but I can tell you, practice is necessary.

In terms of practicality, having your questions printed on a sheet of paper is a great idea. This also allows you to take notes as you go through them. I have a brown leather compendium I take to all my first sales meetings and it contains only four things in it:

1. three copies of my first sales meeting questions

2. a one-page diagram of the steps in The Infinite Sales System printed on thick stock

3. an A5 size note pad

4. a mechanical pencil. (I'm left handed ... if you know, you know.)

When I'm back in my office after a first sales meeting (or if I finish one online), I remove the copy of the questions from the folder that includes all my notes, and replace it with a new one, so I always have three in there at any time. (I have about 10 printed off next to my desk, so I can always grab new ones quickly.)

During your first sales meeting, it's completely okay for your prospects to see you're following a list of questions; in fact, it's encouraged. This shows you're a professional and following a process, which is the opposite of making it up as you go. This should impress your prospects — plus, it means you never have to memorise your questions.

Even after all this time, if you asked me what my nine questions are off the top of my head, I would usually be able to recall eight of them, but I seem to forget a different one each time! So, again, you don't have to remember your first sales meeting questions because you'll always have them in front of you in the meeting.

FAQ

Q: Isn't it rude to be taking notes in front of someone?

A: Quite the opposite. Taking notes (on paper rather than a device) is a sign of respect and it shows you're paying attention.

PICKING UP IMPORTANT CLUES

While I'm taking the prospect through my open questions, a lot of information is coming at me. In my mind, I'm constantly sifting through all this information like a detective and searching for the answers to the four questions that will help me to determine my probability of moving the conversation forward. These four questions are:

- Do they have a problem?

- How big is their problem?

- What is their appetite for solving their problem?

- Are we the right people to serve them?

DO THEY HAVE A PROBLEM?

Unless your prospect is aware of their problem, you have little chance of converting them. It's like the person who is unhealthy and overweight but continues sailing through life without a care in the world. Until they can admit they have a problem, you're going to have a hard time getting them to change their lifestyle.

HOW BIG IS THEIR PROBLEM?

This is about your assessment of how serious the problem is (not their awareness of it). Following on from the previous analogy about the overweight person, do you deem them slightly overweight, or are they morbidly obese and at risk of imminent heart failure?

In my world, I might assess that the problems I could help the prospects out with are relatively minor — for example, their staff need to brush up their skills, they are losing a few contracts here and there on price, or around 15 per cent of their proposals are not converting. I'd consider these small problems.

If, on the other hand, they say they are continually losing contracts on price, or their overall conversion ratio is <30 per cent, or they are continually taking any clients, rather than the right client ... then there is a large problem. (By the way — price is rarely the reason that converts don't convert. More on this in chapter 8.)

WHAT IS THEIR APPETITE FOR SOLVING THEIR PROBLEM?

An appetite to actually solve the problem is an important factor, because it gives you an idea of how ready and willing your prospects are to work with you.

Continuing the previous analogy, say the overweight person has been diagnosed as morbidly obese. If they just suffered a heart attack — and have perhaps just woken up in hospital, rigged up to a dozen beeping machines, surrounded by their two young kids and partner — they are (hopefully!) going to be more willing to want to immediately overhaul their life choices and start eating healthy food, exercising more and looking after themselves properly.

If this same person is still sailing through life with an attitude of, 'Well, I could probably make better choices, but it's not really a problem I need to address', you're going to have a more difficult time convincing them to make changes.

The same thought process applies for your prospects. If they aren't too bothered by their problem or don't even see it as an issue, you're going to have a hard time converting (and convincing) them to work with you.

If you diagnose a serious problem in the company and they don't agree, you're going to have to work hard to convert those prospects. You'll have to find other ways to explain the problem, or perhaps find other 'champions' within the company to help support the cause. This is risky, though, because at this stage of the process, you should only be dealing with the decision-maker, and if they aren't aware of the problem and don't have a high appetite to solve it, you're in for a challenge.

If they are problem aware and have a reasonable appetite to solve it, you're at least talking the same language.

ARE WE THE RIGHT PEOPLE TO SERVE THEM?

This element is as much about your *compatibility* to work together as it is as much about your *desire* to want to work together.

Many businesses have experienced situations where they have seen signs early on that a prospect might be hard work as a client, but they have ignored that instinct and taken them on anyway. They often go on to regret this later. Or it might be that the problem the prospect wants to solve isn't really in your wheelhouse, or is not quite what you do. Or they have a small problem, and your company only tackles big problems. Reflecting on this question allows you to assess both a choice and a fit to work together.

CHECKING YOUR ANSWERS

In terms of these four questions, if you don't achieve a tick in all four boxes, either your conversation is a non-starter or you proceed at your own risk.

Let me share an example from early on in my company. I had a prospect who, against my better judgement, I signed them up — and who, of course, turned out to be the wrong client for me. In measuring this prospect against the four questions:

- *Did they have a problem?* Yes!

- *How big was their problem?* It was spectacularly big.

- *What was their appetite for solving the problem?* Also huge — they were desperate to have a sales process across their company.

- *Was I the right person to serve them?* This was the point I came undone. One of the people I was selling to was disrespectful towards me, was continually distracted in our conversations and, in general, just wasn't my kind of person. I knew it and chose to ignore that all the same because I wanted to help them. It turned out poorly for me, because I didn't enjoy working with them, and found myself anxious prior to conversations with them because they were often unpredictable.

Instead of saying yes to this prospect, I should have assessed them against the four criteria properly, which would have had me respectfully decline the opportunity by sharing how I was unable to assist with their requirements.

You can also use the following scale (see figure overleaf) to assess where the prospects sits in terms of size of problem and awareness. Just remember to also assess whether you are the right person to serve them.

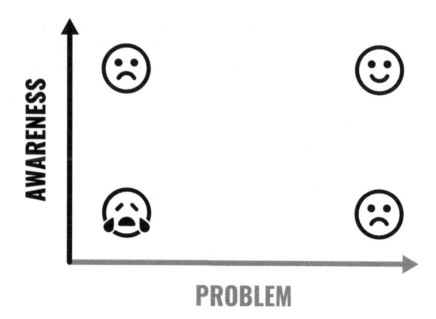

PROBLEM

Also be aware that a prospect's appetite for solving the problem can change because of your first sales meeting. Reflect back on the qualification question process from the previous chapter for a moment. One of the questions that you should have asked at that stage relates to timing and your prospects' level of urgency to solve the particular problem. So up-front, before you even meet them, you should have an idea of their appetite. But this can change. Let me share how this works in my company.

In relation to the question about urgency or timing in my qualification process, fewer than 20 per cent of my prospects answer:

This is our single most important priority right now.

And about 50 per cent answer:

We know we have a problem and are looking for a solution in the next three to six months.

The remaining 30 per cent answer:

We are just gathering information at this stage.

I'm happy to meet with prospects, even if they are just gathering information. Then, during the first sales meeting, I understand more about their situation and I often find that by the end of the meeting, they have now moved to one of the other, more urgent options.

  One of the first rules of negotiation is that if someone is talking to you, then to some degree, you have something that they want. Otherwise, if they have absolutely no interest in what you are selling, they won't even agree to meet with you.

I had a prospect in a large company who started the first sales meeting by telling me, 'Julia, I just wanted to let you know up-front that we will never have a need for your services.'

What's slightly amusing about this story is that this opportunity came about through someone hearing me on a podcast. That person reached out to me, happened to be in my state, and we met for coffee. They worked in a senior role at one of the biggest consulting firms in the world, and thought that their manager might like to meet me to see how I could help them.

Recalling my own corporate experience working at global companies, I had insight into how slow and complicated decision-making can be at companies of this size. So, I managed my own expectations and didn't by any means put all my prospecting eggs in their basket.

In all honesty, I was really interested in converting this opportunity because I thought it would take up a lot of my time, with lots of chasing and numerous decision-makers.

Side point: When I shared with some *friends* that I had an opportunity to discuss my services with this company, they were all amazed and asked me about how I might prepare for the big 'pitch meeting', how much research I was going to do and what special things I might bring along to impress them.

When I shared about this opportunity with my *clients*, however, and I asked them how I was going to prepare for such an opportunity as this one, they all knew the answer — no different to how I approach any other prospect. The process never changes.

I must confess that I'm a 'deal junkie', though, so when the decision-maker started the meeting by rejecting me, an internal switch flicked on, and my first thought was, *Challenge accepted!*

Now, considering that first rule of negotiation I just mentioned, what have you learned? Yes, that's right. Something didn't add up. Why would a very senior manager at this very large company accept a one-hour meeting with someone who they had no intention of ever working with?

So, I followed my signature framework for objection handling (look forward to chapter 8 for more on that topic), and applied two seconds of silence. I then curiously delivered, 'Huh, that's interesting. Can you tell me some more about that?'

Plot twist: I converted them and it took only four weeks to do so.

I had a laugh about this with the person who made that statement after we started working together. I asked if they remembered saying it to me and then, in my cheeky style, said, 'Look how that worked out!' We both laughed.

I tie off this section of the first sales meeting with a reminder to take your time in asking your open questions. Accept this takes time, and don't rush this part.

Just follow the process. Do the things.

Deliver your summary statements

After you have asked your open questions, you now need to transition the conversation and demonstrate you have captured what is important to your prospect.

By now in your first sales meeting, you've spent a lot of time listening, applying strategic silence and learning all about your prospect's situation. You've also likely taken a lot of notes.

What this component is *not* about is summarising everything you've heard in the conversation so far. This would take way too long. What you need to do instead is play back some short statements showing you have listened, you've captured the brief and you appreciate what is important to your prospects.

As you're working your way through your open questions, particular topics will hit a metaphorical 'hot button' with your prospect. More often than not, these topics relate to negative issues or problems — for example, losing revenue, poor team engagement, low margins, losing customers, or reduced competitive advantage, market share or competitive activity.

When you hear your prospect talk about instances like this, don't just make a note about it — mark an asterisk next to it.

Once you've conducted your open questions, you should be able to identify around three to five big ticket items (or 'hot buttons') that are important to your prospect or to the organisation. Those three to five elements will form the basis for your summary statements.

Here's the format to use when sharing your summary statements:

1. Introduction to summary statements:
   a. Thank you for sharing so much with me.
   b. Do you mind if I play some of that back to ensure I've captured the main points?

2. Short statements, starting with:
   a. It looks like ...
   b. It feels like ...
   c. It sounds like ...
   d. It seems like ...
   e. What I'm hearing is ...

3. Confirmation:
   a. Have I captured that correctly, or have I missed something?

Importantly, don't use language like, 'You said X', or 'You told me Y'. This kind of language can be received as confrontational and accusatory, which you want to avoid.

By using the recommended statements just provided, your language is softer, and you leave margin for someone to correct you if you are off course.

When delivering summary statements with competence and then finishing with the confirmation statement provided, you'll usually find your prospect will respond with something along the lines of, 'Yes! That's right.'

This affirmative response always amuses me, because frequently it is delivered with enthusiasm, or even surprise that I got it right.

I think to myself, *I don't know why they are so surprised. I'm only playing back what they already told me!* I've learned people respond this way, however, because they are accustomed to people not properly listening. So when I deliver these summary statements, they feel heard, possibly for the first time ever.

This is why this technique is not to be underestimated — it reinforces the very satisfaction of feeling understood and being heard.

Another important point about summary statements is that you're not simply repeating phrases your prospects have used. Let me give you some examples to illustrate this point. My prospects might share with me something like, 'We aren't working with the right types of clients', 'We experience inconsistent revenue' or, 'We work in a competitive industry and find it hard to stand out'. I read *beyond* this information and transform it into powerful summary statements using the framework just provided.

So instead of playing back:

> *It seems like you aren't working with the right types of clients.*

I play back:

> *I'm hearing that you want your team to be really leveraging their skills by working with larger clients who will reward you with higher margins.*

And instead of playing back:

> *It feels like you are frustrated because your revenue isn't consistent.*

I play back:

It feels like inconsistent revenue is holding you back from accurately forecasting the business, which makes it impossible to see your financial future or make financial decisions around staffing, investment or marketing spend.

And instead of playing back:

It sounds like you have many competitors also vying for the same prospects.

I play back:

It sounds like you're having to reduce your margins to win business because you're trying to stand out in a competitive space. And when you do this, it seems you're doing the same amount of work, but for less revenue.

Put yourself in the position of this prospect for a moment. Can you see why they might now respond with enthusiasm and say, 'Yes! That's right!'?

Summary statements are an incredibly powerful way of showing any human (prospect or otherwise) you've listened, you've captured the brief, and you appreciate what is important to them.

Just pick three to five big-ticket items to summarise and resist the temptation to summarise everything.

Keep it simple. Just do the things.

Outline your hero statement

Blink and you'll miss this part!

Here is where you start to make a transition from the 'about them', to the 'about you' part of the first sales meeting. At this point, you make a short and simple statement that gives your prospect confidence you can help them.

It goes like this:

> *Well, based on what I've learned so far, Aisyah, I'd like to share that we can help you with this.*

This step is important, because it can fill your prospect with confidence that they are talking to the right person, and you have a solution. The statement also helps to transition the conversation into how you can help them.

Keep in mind that your prospect may have tried to solve their challenges previously through other means — and yet, here they are, with problems still unsolved. If you've ever experienced back pain, you probably know what this is like. You may have had to visit a bunch of doctors, physiotherapists or specialists, before finally finding 'the one' who can tell you, 'I appreciate your pain and I'm the right person to help you fix it'. Such a statement can fill you with confidence (and relief).

This small step in the process does exactly the same thing. It allows your prospect to feel at ease that help is on the way.

That's it. Keep it simple. Just do the things.

Highlight the emotional benefits

This element of your first sales meeting is one of the key components that can reward you with competitive advantage. And the more of a competitive industry you operate in, the more of an impact this section will have on your ability to stand out.

Highlighting the *emotional* benefits of working with your business, shifts the way you talk about your products and services, and makes someone sit up and pay attention to you. It has the ability to move you from being a 'nice to have', to a 'need'.

 ## Sell the problem you solve, not the product you sell.

Consider this statement for a moment. What do you think it really means?

When it comes to explaining products or services, so many professionals focus on explaining the 'what' component rather than the 'how'. So they talk a lot about how great their customer service is, how experienced their team are, the number of awards they have won, what other customers say about them or their high standards of work.

Plot twist: Your prospect doesn't care about this.

Instead, what they care about is how they will benefit from working with you and what problems you can solve for them. Your product or service is simply the vehicle you're both using to solve their problems.

We are all consumers, and we're all human, so the person you're selling to (your prospect) is a person just like you. For the most part, we all have similar problems and challenges in our lives, so when we can find ways to make those go away, the solution becomes easy to buy.

Imagine I had some kind of magic potion that was (safely and legitimately) able to keep your family and children healthy and happy for a lifetime. (As far-fetched as this sounds, stay with me. We are imagining!) If this safe potion was legitimate and you knew it could save your family from pain, sickness and distress, would you want it? Would you buy it? What price would you put on such a potion?

If it were me, I would want it. I'd definitely buy it and I'd probably be prepared to pay quite a lot for it, knowing the problems it would solve for me. Once I trusted that the potion was safe, I'd be less concerned about exactly what ingredients were in it, and more focused on the outcome I was about to achieve.

In this example, the potion is the *vehicle* I'm using to achieve health and happiness for my family.

Now consider your own life for a moment. What are some everyday problems or challenges you'd like to solve? Perhaps you'd like to get paid more, work less, spend more time with your family, enjoy more holidays, stress less, sleep better, have more time for hobbies and have good health — any of these take your fancy? These are called *emotional benefits*, because they change the way we feel.

If you were to ask the same question of the person you are selling to, they will likely come up with a very similar list of emotional benefits. They may also add some commercial benefits in there based on the problems they would like to solve — such as increasing market share, mitigating risk or gaining competitive advantage — which would also have some emotional benefits behind them.

The emotional benefits are the outputs your product or service needs to deliver to your prospect.

So rather than talk about all the features, inclusions and attributes of your product or service, shift the way you talk about them to link directly to these outputs.

As an example from my own company, the *vehicle* I'm selling is a repeatable sales process called The Infinite Sales System.

I could provide prospects with details on the following features, inclusions and attributes:

- how long it goes for

- how many hours each session is

- what the workbook looks like

- when it runs

- what the individual modules involve

- who from my team will run which module.

But I don't. Instead, I focus the conversation on how The Infinite Sales System can help them increase market share, save time, make money and gain competitive advantage. This makes for a much more compelling reason to partner with me. It also follows the theme of this process and continues to make the conversation more about someone else, and less about me.

I've actually had clients shed tears when they learn this module because, for the first time ever, they can explain their point of difference in such a compelling way. It's been pivotal for many clients — so much so that many go on to use the work from this module and update the language on their website and all their marketing materials.

As always, don't try to just wing it with this element. Really nailing the emotional benefits of your offering requires some preparation:

1. Review the list of emotional benefits provided earlier in this section (such as working and stressing less, and spending more time with family), and highlight the ones that your product or service can address for your potential customer. For example, do your clients benefit from saving money, reducing their risk or saving time when they partner with you?

2. Demonstrate why or how your product or service will help them achieve this outcome through a few short statements.

The following examples highlight how this might work in practice.

EXAMPLE 1: YOU'RE A LEADERSHIP CONSULTANCY FIRM

You identify the following emotional benefits you can provide by helping your prospect solve their identified problems:

- save time

- save money

- increase market share.

You now need to demonstrate why or how your product or service will help them achieve these benefits.

SAVE TIME

Here's how you highlight the benefit of saving time:

I realise we're talking about leadership consulting services [the 'vehicle'] here; however, when you partner with our organisation, what you're really going to benefit from is saving time across your organisation:

- *Through our unique leadership skills development program, your leaders will be enabled and better equipped to handle challenges swiftly and effectively, reducing the time spent on problem-solving and conflict resolution.*

- *And through implementing our change management strategies, you will accelerate transition periods and reduce the time your company spends adapting to new processes or structures.*

SAVE MONEY

And saving money:

We'll also help you to save money through partnering with us because:

- *You'll enjoy enhanced leadership skills, which directly contributes to a more motivated and engaged workforce. So you will reduce employee turnover.*

- *By investing in leadership development, your company can save significantly on the costs associated with hiring and training new staff, because you'll have top quality staff who will stay with your organisation for longer.*

- *By training your leaders in data-driven decision-making, your company can avoid costly mistakes and missed opportunities. Leaders who can interpret data accurately and make informed decisions are less likely to commit resources to unprofitable projects or activities.*

GAIN A COMPETITIVE ADVANTAGE

And gaining a competitive advantage:

You'll also achieve competitive advantage *when you partner with us because:*

- *Your team will transform into high-performing business units by driving a culture of accountability, efficiency and mutual respect, directly impacting your bottom line.*

- *This will also increase your reputation in the market place, helping you win higher profile projects so you become the preferred supplier within your industry.*

EXAMPLE 2: YOU'RE AN IT COMPANY

You identify the following emotional benefits for your prospect:

- save money

- mitigate risk.

You now need to highlight why or how your product or service will help them achieve this.

SAVE MONEY

Here's how you talk about the benefit of saving money:

I realise we're talking about IT services [the 'vehicle'] here; however, when you partner with our organisation, what you're really going to benefit from is saving money *across your organisation:*

- *How we can help you do that is by conducting a comprehensive audit that will allow us to consolidate underutilised technology with platforms you're already paying for, so you'll avoid duplication.*

- *You'll also enjoy increased productivity p/hour through automating parts of your team's roles, so they can spend less time on manual processes and more time growing existing accounts.*

MITIGATE RISK

And mitigating risk:

We will also help you mitigate risk *because:*

- *Your cyber security will be upgraded to ensure protection from external threats, which can be crippling for businesses.*

- *You'll also have peace of mind that your customer data is protected and not open for exposure, which can result in reputational damage.*

- *You'll reduce downtime and risk of outages because of our comprehensive and industry-leading backup protocols.*

What you are aiming for here is a series of short statements you can refer to that directly relate to the problems your prospect is trying to solve.

These statements directly address the problem your prospect is looking to solve, and create a much more compelling reason to partner with you than simply telling them about how experienced your team are, and the high standard of work you produce. Don't be tempted to delve into the details on your products or services, yet.

Keep it simple. Just do the things. (Are you starting to see the pattern here?)

Make recommendations

This is the moment you've been waiting for — where you can talk about you, finally!

By now, you've spent a lot of time listening to the issues at hand, learning what is important to your prospect, and showing them they have been heard, and how you comprehend the brief.

You're now ready to make some recommendations — but this element of the first sales meeting comes with a few subsections.

Firstly, at this point you can ask all your technical and logistical questions that will help you to build a proposal or give a quote. In chapter 4, I cover how these questions are 'transactional questions', and they are about the stuff and the things (very technical!). You can ask questions here about delivery, time frames, personnel, budgets, materials, logistics or other details. You can think of these questions almost like 'check-box' questions about the data and information required for you to provide a proposal.

Secondly, you can share more about your company and services. The key is to keep this succinct — because time is ticking away and you don't want to run overtime!

Do not present them with a comprehensive company history and a list of arduous case studies. You must also avoid presenting your menu of everything you offer. Do you remember why? Well, for two reasons:

- You risk them being confused, and a confused mind always says 'no'. You'll be harder to buy from.

- You won't have time. You're getting to the pointy end of the first sales meeting now, so you don't have time to spend 30 minutes on your company presentation and history.

You may wish to take prospects through your company values and how they relate to how you serve your clients. You might even provide a short history or perhaps a (short) relevant case study that highlights your success on similar projects. You should cover your (relevant) products or services here as well.

In stark contrast to many businesses (and quite likely your business), my company is very easy to buy from, because we have one thing, for one price. I don't offer a menu of options, and I don't slice up the offer to suit the prospect. I realise this isn't possible for all businesses, but it works for mine.

Our program, The Infinite Sales System, is well researched and provided in a way that solves many problems for our clients. In addition, we can confidently assert that this is our recommendation for them if they want to solve said challenges.

Thirdly, you're now in a position to provide your recommendation — that is, your professional opinion based on your experience and what your prospects have shared with you at this meeting. You might already have a solid idea of how to help them, or you might be able to give some general thoughts on ideas. So let them know either:

- Based on what they shared with you, you can make a recommendation.

- You'd like to have a think about how you can help them, and then you'll put some recommendations together for them.

Finally, let them know you'll send a proposal, which they will receive in the next 24 hours (if that's feasible for your company). If not, let them know when they can expect it from you, and then over-deliver on this deadline.

Remember — it's important to get proposals out as soon as possible, because this continues momentum and shows your prospects you are focused on them.

FAQ

Q: Do I talk about our prices at this stage, or should we just put them in the proposal?

A: It's helpful to at least give a ballpark figure or range on your price if possible at this stage. If you do have an idea and you present it to them, and they then express a difference on budget, you want to know this now. Similarly, if this ends up being a non-starter because of price, you want to know immediately.

Outline next steps

I need a megaphone for this section, so if you've been reading this book before bed and are about to nod off, I suggest you put it down now and go to sleep. Come back when you're revived and ready for this next section, because this element is the biggest game-changer in The Infinite Sales System. You cannot afford to miss any part of it!

If you act on only one element from this program, let *this* be it. This is the single, most important factor that will determine if your proposal goes down the route of floating around in space, or if you convert the opportunity.

Here it is:

 # Never finish a meeting without booking in the next meeting.

Say it with me — never finish a meeting without booking in the next meeting.

Now, take that phrase and put it on 47 sticky notes in your office, in your car and next to your computer, or go get a tattoo with it. I think you get my point. ☺

This is the only element across the entirety of The Infinite Sales System where you'll kick yourself for forgetting it.

Before your meeting wraps up, you're going to take an active step to keep the process moving forward. If you skip this step, your process will not move forward and you risk it going backwards and losing the opportunity.

Here's what you're going to say:

> *It's been great chatting with you today, Rana. I'm going to send you a summary of what we've spoken about today along with our recommendations, and I'll have that with you by tomorrow morning. Then you can look over that in your own time.*

You know what we should do, though? Let's keep the momentum going on our conversation and book in for a short chat later next week, just for 10 to 15 minutes so I can see how this is sitting with you. I've got my calendar handy, do you have yours?'

Then, you'll whip out your phone calendar on the spot, agree to a time and send the calendar appointment to them immediately. This meeting should be conducted online via a Zoom or Teams meeting, because it's not productive to drive to visit your prospect for a 15-minute meeting.

Conducting this online also sets the tone of a check-in, and 15 minutes is not an unreasonable ask of your prospect.

My clients achieve 100 per cent of first sales meetings with a second sales meeting booked in, and you should too, using this technique.

This is not my first rodeo and I can tell you, if you loosely agree to catch up in the next few weeks, I know how that ends. You're going to be chasing them and wondering why they aren't returning your calls, which is a horrible feeling and a giant waste of your time.

Over the years, I've had countless clients joke with me about producing a range of merchandise (maybe coffee cups or caps) with what they have called my 'Julia-isms' on it. One of the Julia-isms they talk about is the following statement: 'I've got my calendar handy, do you have yours?'

All my clients have heard me and my staff use that phrase hundreds of times, so it's now ingrained in them as well!

Plot twist: There will not be merch. 😊

FAQ

Q: I don't think my prospects will agree to locking in a second meeting. Isn't it pushy to ask for a second sales meeting?

A: Not at all! First, in The Infinite Sales System, no one is pushing anyone for anything. This is a process about helping people move closer towards solving their challenge. Second, you're helping the process to move forward with this step. It shows you're dedicated to helping them with a solution. Gaining that second sales meeting really is as a simple as assuming it's going ahead, and booking it in. You're not asking for permission to have a second meeting, but showing them this is your process. Following process gives you a higher degree of professionalism. Follow the process. If you do, 99 per cent will agree (if not 100 per cent), so just do the things. 😊

First sales meeting: Splitting up the pie

You now have all the elements of your first sales meeting — congratulations! In this section, I break up the meeting so you know how much time to spend on each element.

Remember — your first sales meeting goes for one hour, and it includes a number of elements. The following figure shows a rough plan of how many minutes to allocate to each element.

FIRST SALES MEETING TIME

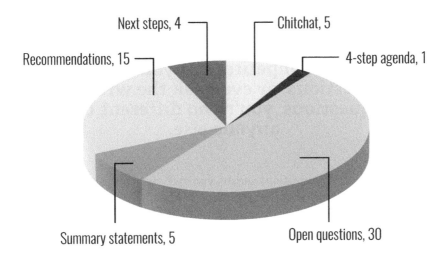

Next steps, 4 — Chitchat, 5

Recommendations, 15 — 4-step agenda, 1

Summary statements, 5 — Open questions, 30

You'll notice the open-questions component takes up the bulk of the meeting. This section should go for 30 to 40 minutes, and here's the pro tip for you: resist the temptation to skip questions. I know you'll want to, but don't. I've seen this happen enough times for me to warn you about it (again!).

I know that you know how to help your prospect. In fact, they also probably know that you know how to help them. That's why they're meeting with you.

However, if you skip the questions or you cut this element down to 15 minutes, you risk being seen as approaching them 'competence first', rather than 'trust first'. And our lesson from Amy Cuddy (back in chapter 4) suggests if you do this, you're not going to build trust.

A first sales meeting is designed to be an experience for your prospects, and an opportunity for them to view you as more professional than any of your competitors. If you skip the questions, or even ask the wrong questions, you're no different to anyone else.

Skipping the open questions means you risk two things:

- being perceived as expensive, because you're not offering anything unique

- losing trust — and we all know where that ends.

In my first sales meeting, my 'recommendations' come at about the 45th minute and go for around four minutes. You'll notice I've allocated 15 minutes in the previous figure for this step, but I'm able to get it down to four. First, as I mentioned earlier, this is a little easier for me because I only have one thing that I'm selling for one price. But, regardless, you should always keep this section as succinct as possible. With time and practice, you too might be able to get it down to just four minutes.

I stick to the process, and it doesn't change. I just do the things.

Putting the first sales meeting together

Now you have the entire framework for your first sales meeting, so let's put it together. Remember, in real time, this meeting goes for an hour. As you read through the following, it may seem like a lot of words from you, but remember that you will have a lot of interactive dialogue coming back at you. The prospect should be talking a lot more than you.

For this example, let's imagine you're an architect meeting with a prospect. You kick off your meeting with some informal chitchat, and then steer the meeting with something like the following:

So, Min, I'd like to respect your time, so shall we get started?

> *I've come prepared today to ask you some questions, so I can learn about your situation and what you're looking to achieve. Based on what you share with me, I'll be able to make some recommendations or even give you some advice. Then, we can agree on any next steps. Does that sound okay with you?*

[Open questions:]

> *Okay, so why don't you kick off by telling me about your latest project in terms of the architecture component?*
>
> *What's been your experience working with architects previously?*
>
> *Can you tell me about how important your architect is in this project?*
>
> *What has worked well previously when working with architects?*
>
> *What frustrations have you experienced when working with architects?*

What do you see as the difference between a good architect and a great architect?

If we were to work together, how would we measure our success?

What is your decision-making process in choosing the right architect for this project?

How will you know if you've chosen the right one?

What is the impact of getting this right?

Assuming you're enthusiastic about our conversation today, what would be the next steps from your end?

What barriers might we run into that would stop this conversation moving forward?

Who else will be involved in this decision but isn't here with us today?

How can I make it easy for you to partner with us?

[Summary statements:]

Thanks for sharing all that with me. Do you mind if I play some of that back to ensure I've heard what's important to you?

It seems like you've been burned by architects in the past and you're looking for a better partnership this time where you have more transparency of progress.

It sounds like this project is crucial for your company because you're looking for a design that will boost your reputation for these kinds of builds in the future.

I'm hearing that you are under pressure to protect your margin, which means you are really looking at price as an important factor.

It appears this project has to deliver on time and under budget — otherwise, your next projects will be pushed back for the year.

Have I captured all the main points here or have I missed something?

[Hero statement:]

I want to let you know up-front that this is exactly the kind of work our firm does.

[Emotional benefits:]

I realise we're talking about architecture services here; however, when you partner with our firm what you're really doing is saving time. You'll achieve that with us because we are specialists in the kind of design you're seeking, and we've completed numerous projects in this field previously, so you will minimise the number of revisions it will take for us to help realise your vision, which means you'll commence your project faster.

Partnership with us will also allow you to increase your market share, because our design work is award winning, so you will end up with an edgy design that makes you stand out in the marketplace, helping you attract more projects of this scale and type in the future.

And, finally, we'll also help you to save and make money, because we are specialists in this kind of work, so we're confident you'll commence the build faster, meaning you'll be finished ahead of time, allowing you to start making sales on the building faster than you may have done if you worked with someone less experienced who took longer to commence.

What do you make of that so far?

[Recommendations:]

May I ask you now about some of the technical parts of the project, which will help us to put a proposal together?

Let me share with you about our company … [Brief company history and/or case studies here.]

Some initial thoughts we have with this project are … [Possible recommendations here.]

We're going to put something together for you, and we anticipate having that to you by … [Firm date for when the proposal will be sent here.]

[Next steps:]

But you know what we should do? Let's keep the momentum going on our conversation and book in for another conversation in a week or so, just so I can see how this is sitting with you. It's only a short chat, maybe 10 to 15 minutes. I've got my calendar handy, do you have yours?

So that's all the pieces put together!

While that might seem like a lot, the good news is you only have to know one tiny part of the first sales meeting off by heart. Do you remember which component it is?

It's the 4-step agenda, which in real time goes for about 17 seconds.

You can (and should) take your printed sales process with you to every first sales meeting, so you never have to worry about forgetting anything.

When you take someone through your 4-step agenda, you should feel a sense of strength about it, because it shows that you're clearly following a process, which (as covered back in chapter 3) is the exact opposite of making it up as you go.

Now, you wouldn't want to be reading your sales process word for word, so it's imperative you've practised the individual elements over and over again, so they come across as natural and normal.

Your sales process document guides you during the meeting. It's not a script.

Mastering the first sales meeting

Your first sales meeting is important, with many individual elements, but try not to get caught up in thinking you have to conduct each part perfectly the first time. Pick individual parts and build on them each time.

Remember — perfection is the enemy of progress.

As a starting point, learn the 4-step agenda off by heart. As mentioned, in real time, this will take you about 17 seconds so it's not a huge ask for you to learn this.

Then, each subsequent first sales meeting, pick an element you really want to master and concentrate on that. Just do your best with the other elements.

As with learning any other skill, mastering the first sales meeting takes practice.

Pro tip: Most people (not my clients, of course!) won't be disciplined enough to learn and master the individual elements. They will likely give up too quickly and go back to how they used to meet with prospects. Will you be like most people?

Learning is awkward. It feels strange. You think you're doing it wrong, but it is simply a lack of practice. Consider if you suddenly had to write with your opposite hand or drive on the other side of the road (for example, if you were in Europe). At first, it would feel very wrong! But it's not wrong, it's just different.

Stick with the process. I know this works, and my clients know it works. So be like us! Just do the things!

CHAPTER 7

STEP THREE: MEETING FOLLOW UP

Let's assume you've just conducted a fantastic first sales meeting. You covered all the elements outlined in the previous chapter with a high degree of competency. As your prospect departs your meeting, they should be thinking about how great that was, how insightful your questions were, and how much they are looking forward to receiving your proposal.

And then a few moments later, they have to snap back into their main role, and they're checking emails and seeing what they missed in the past hour. They soon might not be thinking about you at all.

Avoiding this is where this next step comes in. Your meeting follow-up allows you to continue the momentum until your second sales meeting (which you will have booked in your first sales meeting).

In this chapter, I run through some important ways to keep yourself front of mind with your prospect.

Transferring notes to your CRM

The first action you need to take is transferring your first sales meeting notes into your CRM. Never fear — you don't need to type everything out! All you're going to do is whip out your phone, take a photo of your notes, and then upload this photo straight into your CRM. Many CRMs have an app you can run off your phone; otherwise, save the photo as a document and upload it when you're back at your desk.

Pro tip: You want to save the photo against the Company or Account record in your CRM, not the Contact record. Contacts can change roles or move on from the company, so saving it against the Company/ Account record means your notes won't get lost.

Next, check off in your CRM that you have completed your first sales meeting. (You should have set up your first tasks and meetings in your CRM as part of the qualification process — jump back to chapter 5 for more.)

You also now need to create a 'deal' or 'opportunity' (depending on your CRM language) in relation to the proposal being sent. Be sure to include:

- estimated close date

- $ value

- stage of the process (proposal sent).

Thank you video

A short time after your meeting, your prospect has likely moved on from thinking about you, so you're going to do something innovative here to surprise and delight them — you're going to send a 'thank you' video.

A short thank you video is a powerful element in The Infinite Sales System because it again demonstrates your point of difference.

Importantly, the thank you video is not a summary of the meeting. It simply does what it says — thanks your prospect. This video should go for about 30 to 45 seconds — if you find yourself babbling on for more than one minute, you need to re-record it! It's meant to be short and pleasant.

The content of this video is simply something like the following:

Hi Matisse — I just wanted to thank you for meeting with me today. I really enjoyed hearing about this new project and it was interesting to learn about [mention something specific]. What I'm going to do from here is put a proposal together with our recommendations, and I'll have that to you by Thursday afternoon. I'll look forward to seeing you again the following Friday. Have a great rest of your week. Bye! 😊

That's all it is. It's a friendly video you will record for each prospect after you conduct your first sales meeting.

Pro tip: Don't record the video on your phone through the usual camera app. Your file size will end up being far too big and you won't be able to email it. Instead, use the free software platform Loom. It's a fantastic platform and easy to use. Once you've recorded your video through Loom, you then send the video as a link, rather than a file.

Another pro tip: Don't send your email with the video link right away. It's too soon. You should record the video as soon as your meeting is over, though — otherwise, you may forget!

Using your email platform, schedule to send the link about four hours after your meeting. If your first sales meeting was in the afternoon, schedule it to send first thing the following morning.

The content of your email should be very short.

Your email subject should be: *Thank you video*

Your email is:

> *Hi Matisse,*
>
> *I've recorded you a short video, which you can click and view here [insert link].*
>
> *Kind regards,*
>
> *Julia*

Avoid the temptation to set up a studio production for your thank you video. It's not meant to be this! It's meant to be a short video to re-engage your prospect again. They won't remember afterwards what you wore or how many times you said 'um' or 'ah', and they won't care where you're sitting or standing!

Just record and send the first take (unless it ends up too long).

Perfection is the enemy of progress, so just keep it simple and do the things.

FAQ

Q: But I don't like recording videos of myself. I could never do this.

A: I hear you. In fact, you're not alone and many clients have told me the exact same thing. As harsh as it sounds, my clients have told me they simply needed to do one thing to start sending the thank you video. They needed to get over themselves. With the hundreds of these that my clients have sent, the response has been overwhelmingly positive. This video is designed to keep your connection going and as highlighted in chapter 4, people buy from people they like. This video makes you more likeable.

Sending your proposal

This section isn't hugely detailed, for a few reasons.

Firstly, because of how you've conducted your first sales meeting, your proposal is no longer the biggest factor in determining whether you win the work or not. By this stage, your prospect already feels like you are better, more trustworthy *and* more competent. Of course, your proposal is still important; however, a lot of the heavy lifting has already been completed — well done!

Secondly, every company is different, and every proposal is different. Some companies have templates, designs or teams who construct proposals.

Irrespective of how your company constructs a proposal, here are some recommendations you may wish to note:

- *Ensure your proposal doesn't commence with being all about your company and your team:* Your prospect doesn't care about you as much as they care about themselves. Leading your proposal with pages and pages about you is not showing them that they are important to you. It's showing them that you're trying to be competent.

- *Start by sharing how you understand their brief:* Use your summary statements and emotional benefit statements to demonstrate how you listened to what was important to them in the first sales meeting.

- *Share your recommendations rather than all the options they can choose from:* They have entered a conversation with you because they are looking for an expert to help them solve a problem. Presenting them with all your products and services makes you hard to buy from. Keep it simple, leverage your experience and share exactly what you see as the solution.

- *Ensure your pricing is clear, and near the top:* They shouldn't have to scroll through 10 pages to find the investment level. Make it clear and obvious. If it does need to slip down a little, put in a table of contents so it's easy to find.

- *Place anything about your company and your team at the end or, even better, attach separately:* If your proposal is too long, you risk making it hard for your prospects to move forward with you. The caveat to this, of course, is if your services are technically complex or if government work is involved. In these cases, you may be required to provide a lengthy document. If it's not essential, though, don't do it.

- *Include any legislative or compliance documents (if needed) as separate attachments:* Again, this ensures they don't need to scroll through multiple pages (in this case, all the legalese) to get to the part they actually want to hear about.

Your proposal should also follow a template structure to increase your efficiency. While each prospect may require individual components of difference, the bulk of your document should be the same.

FAQ

Q: When do I send the proposal?

A: You want to strike while the iron is hot and show your prospects they are a priority to you. So send your proposal within 24 hours wherever possible.

CHAPTER 8

STEP FOUR: THE SECOND SALES MEETING

By the time you get to this step, your prospect has been qualified, participated in a solid first sales meeting, received a thank you video and seen your proposal. Now you're ready to prepare for your second sales meeting.

The structure for this meeting is much more intuitive than the structure for your first sales meeting, because in this meeting you're more likely to be led by your prospect.

This meeting is still absolutely crucial and, when conducted with proficiency, should serve you in the following ways:

- continue the momentum on your conversation and in your quest to help them solve a challenge within their business

- give them an opportunity to share what's on their mind in relation to moving forward with you

- allow you to learn about any reservations (or objections) they have in partnering with you

- ensure they have all the relevant information so they can make an informed decision about what's right for them

- create agreement on where to from here.

Pro tip: Although the second sales meeting is scheduled in your calendars for 15 minutes, be sure to keep your calendar open for the 30 minutes following the meeting. This will mean you have time if they wish to ask more questions or you get caught up in great conversation. If they wish to continue the conversation and you need to dash to your next meeting, you'll stifle the process and lose momentum.

Opening the second sales meeting

Much like the first sales meeting, your second sales meeting commences with some informal chitchat.

Pro tip: In chapter 4, I outline the trust equation, and highlight how important the intimacy component of this equation is. Remember — people buy from people they like, and people are more likely to agree with people they like. Why am I reminding you of this, you may ask? You should always be looking for opportunities to connect and build trust — and should always be prepared to create an opportunity to connect if one doesn't present itself.

When your chitchat begins, it usually kicks off with, 'How are you?' (or similar). Back in chapter 4, I also cover open questions, and show how a question like this doesn't really create much conversation, aside from a token, 'Good thanks. How are you?'

Instead, come prepared to start the chitchat by sharing something personal, but safe and informal. So when you are asked, 'How are you?', you can reply with something like, 'I've had a tough morning with getting the kids to school today', 'I went for my usual cycle this morning, so I'm feeling pretty good' or, 'I had a win this week, so I'm feeling great about the week'.

All of these informal statements lend themselves to opening up the conversation and receiving a follow-up question — for example, about how many kids you have and their age, how far you cycle or what win you had. This helps the casual chitchat turn into opportunities to build connection and move you further up the trust ladder.

Knowing you only have a short time for this meeting, after a few short minutes of chitchat, you can transition into the business conversation using the same first line of the 4-step agenda (from chapter 6): 'I'd like to respect your time again today, so shall we get started?' They should reply with a 'yes', and wait for you to lead.

You can then kick off with an open but direct question like, 'So, tell me what's been on your mind about what we spoke about last week?' or, 'Tell me what you made of our conversation last week?'

What you're trying to achieve from this question is them telling you exactly what their intentions are in relation to your proposal.

Are they intending to:

- proceed now

- proceed possibly at a later date

- modify the scope of your proposal

- clarify parts of your proposal

- never proceed.

You need to know exactly which of these categories your prospects are in, so you know what to do next. This kind of direct questioning should also help them open up on any questions or reservations they have about proceeding with you.

Welcome to objection handling!

Handling objections

This is the part of the sales experience many people favour the least, mostly due to being in a conversation where you risk rejection!

Who really enjoys the feeling of rejection? No-one! That's who!

It's important to accept that objections will present themselves to you, no matter how positive your first meeting or how strong your proposal. You can view them in alternative ways:

- They are not a 'yes', yet.

- They are a request for more information.

- They are an indicator of missing or misunderstood information.

- They are not a rejection of you personally.

- They are almost always because something about your product or service isn't what they are seeing.

Understanding the reasons behind objections

Again, objections are not a personal rejection — and it's up to you to uncover the real reasons behind them.

A famous TED Talk I recommend to all my clients is *'What I learned from 100 days of rejection'* from Jia Jiang. In this short 15-minute video, Jiang outlines his quest to desensitise himself to the feeling of being rejected — by setting himself up to be rejected for 100 days. At the end of these 100 days, he tells us, he hoped to have built his immunity to rejection to the point where he could learn from the experience and become a better person. He was so set on self-improvement that he decided to film himself during these daily interactions and watch the recordings back later to uncover the lessons.

We see him start the social experiment and be terrified the first time he is rejected when asking a stranger to borrow $100. He turns and runs away from the fear! But he later reflects when watching the video that the person who rejected him wasn't really that scary.

In another of his 100 quests, he knocks on the door of a random person and asks if he can plant a flower in their backyard. He is met with immediate rejection and receives a flat 'no'. But, by now, he realises the impact of a powerful word — 'why' — and he asks the reason they said no.

Surprisingly, they didn't say no because of the way he looked or because they didn't trust him. They said no because they had a pet dog who liked to dig up plants! So, in this example, the product simply wasn't the right fit.

You can take two major lessons from Jiang:

1. rejections (and objections) are not about you

2. the conversation becomes much more helpful when you can understand the 'why'.

Handling objections the right way follows the theme of the sales process so far, because it allows you to have a collaborative conversation about the 'why' behind your prospect having reservations. It's not your job to force your product or services down their throats, but it is your job to give them all the relevant information so they can make an informed choice about what's right for them.

  If your prospects have an objection, you likely need to clarify some of your information. You're helping them.

Inviting a collaborative conversation

Irrespective of your business, objections fall into three categories, shown in the following table.

Objection categories

Price	• Budget
	• Value proposition
Product	• Features
	• Fit
	• Personnel or resourcing
	• Materials, colours, service types
Risk	• Timing
	• Market conditions

Objections in all of these categories bring up the potential for some difficult conversations. You may, for example, come up against some hard questions about your price, product, personnel, quality or other terms of business. This is why objection handing has a higher degree of difficulty than other elements of The Infinite Sales System. It requires you to become skilled in The Infinite Sales System Objection Handling Framework, *and* it requires you to step into these potentially difficult conversations.

If you are terrified of difficult conversations and have no interest in learning how to manage them better, I have some good news for you! I can share a simple strategy with you, and then you can skip the rest of this chapter and read ahead to the next chapter.

The strategy for you is this: when you are met with objections (especially about your price), just drop your price to whatever price your prospect wants to pay and agree to anything and everything your prospect asks you to change about your proposal. ☺

Easy! Now you get to avoid the difficult conversation ... but something tells me you realise by now this really isn't what you should be doing!

So if you've decided to read on and *not* skip this chapter, I have some more good news for you.

The way I'm going to teach you to handle objections will feel much more collaborative and much less uncomfortable ... but you will need to step into the conversation. Stay with me, though — I know if you don't skip this chapter, you'll be happy you stayed!

When I talk about objection handling, I mean simply allowing yourself an opportunity to troubleshoot and answer questions. Conducted correctly, you get to avoid the conflict and the conversation feels very productive. Conducted incorrectly, the conversation feels pressured. You risk making someone feel uncomfortable and may even get into conflict.

Let me show you what objection handling is not:

Prospect: *Your company seems great, but your price is just higher than we thought.*

You: *Yes, but the reason our price is higher is because we manufacture locally, rather than offshore.*

Prospect: *Yes, but even then, your competitors are priced 6 per cent lower and that's what we have been used to paying.*

You: *Yes, but we are the only company who manufacture locally, and our team are the most experienced in this kind of work.*

Prospect: *Yes, but we don't have the budget for that much.*

You: *Yes, but ...*

Prospect: *Yes, but ...*

You: *Yes, but ...*

And now we're a hop, skip and a jump away from conflict, because neither person is truly listening to the other and the phrase 'yes, but' implies 'you're wrong and here's why'. This is the opposite of having a collaborative conversation.

Instead, you want to shift the way you even set up this conversation so you invite collaboration and information sharing.

Getting this right has two parts:

1. respond, don't react

2. explore the details.

In the first part of this process, you are purposefully slowing down the conversation once you recognise an objection has presented itself. Now, this sounds simple, but it isn't easy.

This is the difference between responding and reacting. Reacting is hearing, 'Your price is higher than all your competitors' and jumping in with, 'Yes, but that's because ...' Instead, you need to respond calmly, saying something along the lines of, 'Huh, that's interesting. Can you tell me more about that?'

This response completely changes the way you enter into an objection handling conversation. In the same way, you can use the respond technique when someone disagrees with you. Again, doing so promotes collaboration rather than confrontation with how you progress from here.

The elements to follow in this step are:

- *Pause:* Take two seconds to recognise the disagreement or objection, and catch yourself before you react.

- *Clarify:* Ask a simple question designed to get them to share more information.

- *Zero-in:* Check if they wish to object to any other elements, or have other concerns.

These elements are shown in the following figure.

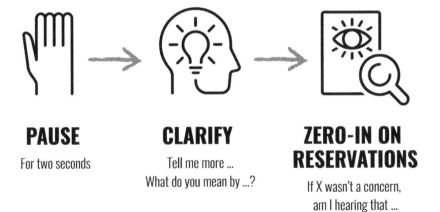

PAUSE
For two seconds

CLARIFY
Tell me more ...
What do you mean by ...?

ZERO-IN ON RESERVATIONS
If X wasn't a concern,
am I hearing that ...

Let's look at how this might play out. Say your prospect suggested that now isn't the right time to move forward. Your response would sound something like the following:

[Pause]

Huh, that sounds interesting. Could you share more about what you mean?

Okay, so I'm hearing that if the timing was right, then you'd be happy to move the conversation forward?

Or if they objected to the price, it might sound something like:

[Pause]

Hmmm, okay. Can you tell me more about that?

Right, so it sounds like if we could agree on the price, you'd be happy to continue the conversation. Is that right?

When you respond in this way, you invite your prospect to share more detail around their reservation, and they feel valued because you are inviting their objection, rather than combatting or shutting it down.

Exploring the details

By this stage of the second meeting, your prospects have shared with you the concerns they have and the rationale behind these concerns. If they have multiple concerns, you need to make a note of each one — because you're going to troubleshoot each of them, one at a time.

If they have concerns around pricing, the timing of the project and the materials you have recommended, for example, you would seek permission to talk through each of these three items, ensuring you don't move on to the next one until you have reached agreement on the current item. This conversation can be set up, again in a collaborative way, by asking permission to talk through each item.

Pro tip: Because you're setting up this conversation in a collaborative way, your prospect now has the chance to mention if they can stay a little longer than the 15 minutes allocated for this meeting or needs to rush off. Bringing this up before starting the conversation gives your prospect the choice, and I've never had a prospect say it's an issue. They've always agreed to have the conversation.

In real time, this might feel slow. It's meant to be this way. If you jump to giving your solutions too quickly, you'll miss key information or small insights your prospects place value on and your agreement won't be as solid.

During objection handling, it's important to approach the conversation like you're solving a technical problem.

Come at the objection from an angle of trying to get to the root cause of the problem by asking high-quality questions. The following are some examples:

- If we were priced the same as our competitors, who would be your preferred partner (and why)?

- What is the impact of you pushing back the timing of the project?

- Share with me your thoughts on pricing versus accepting lower-grade materials?

- How long would be an acceptable time for you to push this solution back?

- What is this problem holding you back from achieving?

Years ago, I was in a situation where I was challenged on my price. I had presented my prospect with my fee of $40 000 and they'd responded with surprise, exclaiming this was more than they had in mind. In fact, their initial comment was, 'That's outrageous!'

Rather than jump in and react, and start to defend my price, I recognised this as an objection. So I paused, and replied with, 'Huh, okay. Can you tell me a little more about that?' To which they shared my fee was extraordinarily higher than anyone else they had come across for sales-type programs. I zeroed in by asking, 'Do you mind if I ask you, if pricing wasn't a concern, what other reservations might you have about engaging me for this work?'

Here's how the conversation then played out:

Prospect: *Oh none! It's just that price is so high.*

Me: *Okay, thank you for sharing this. So if I'm hearing you correctly, it sounds like if we could agree on a price, you'd be happy to move forward with me, is that right?*

Prospect: *Yes! I just can't justify paying that much.*

Me: *Okay, well, price is very important, so we should talk about this some more. Would it be okay if we took a few moments to troubleshoot this?*

Prospect: *Of course.*

Me: *Can I ask you, then, what price do you think is reasonable for this work?*

Prospect: *Around $20 000 is what we had thought this would be.*

Me: *Interesting. May I ask how you came up with this amount?*

Prospect: *Well, that's what we've been paying the sales trainer we've used for the last few years.*

Now, if I pause this conversation for just a moment and step outside of it, you might be able to see my prospect has just *gifted me* a crucial piece of information. Can you work out what it is?

If they have been using a particular sales trainer for a number of years previously, then something must not be working — because, otherwise, why are they talking to me?!

Once I learned this vital piece of knowledge, my confidence lifted a little, because I thought if that existing trainer was amazing, we wouldn't even be in conversation. So they were obviously looking to make a change in service providers.

Back to our conversation:

Me: *Okay then. Can I ask, hypothetically, if I were priced the same as your existing trainer, who would your preferred partner be for this service?*

Prospect: *Oh, we'd love to work with you, Julia!*

Me: *Oh, wow. Thank you for saying that! Can you tell me why that's the case?*

Prospect: *Because I've heard so many great things about you. One of my senior leaders previously worked at a company where they brought you in and they said you were terrific, you have experience in this industry ...*

Me: *Why else?*

Prospect: *The learning outcomes you shared with us are so detailed. And the existing trainer we've been using, the team don't really like them that much and their skills seem a bit basic ...*

Me: *Why else?*

Prospect: *Even the process you've taken us through so far has been so professional ... So, all those reasons.*

Me: *Thanks again for saying all that. So, we're talking about a difference here of $20 000. I wonder if I could ask, what would it mean if I wasn't able to change my price? Is this a walk away?*

Prospect: *Well, I don't know if it's a walk away. This price is just so high.*

Me: *I just wonder ... you mention that I'm your preferred choice because of [ALL the reasons provided, which I list back to them] I wonder if you'd be willing to continue with what seems like a less superior offer, just for the sake of $20 000.*

Prospect: *...*

Me: *[Saying nothing]*

Prospect: *...*

Me: *[Saying nothing]*

Prospect: *Okay then, well, let's move forward with this — on one condition.*

Me: *What would that be?*

Prospect: *I don't know what you just did there, but you need to teach it to my team because they discount all the time!* 😊

This part of the conversation does feel slow, but more than anything it should feel calm. It should allow both you and your prospect time to think, reflect, pause and respond.

What's interesting is that when I've shared that story with people, almost everyone tells me I just should have discounted and avoided the difficult conversation. But in that instance, this was a $20 000 conversation and a $40 000 opportunity, so it was completely worth the investment.

Handling objections does require an appetite to step into that conversation.

As I mentioned earlier in this chapter, you can simply avoid any discomfort by discounting at the first sign of hesitation. However, doing so is not good business practice — and it's also not great for your confidence.

In real time, this objection handling conversation might go for 5 minutes (perhaps a little longer if your prospect has multiple concerns). So although it may seem slow as you read through this, in real time, it will feel progressive and constructive.

FAQ

Q: So, are we allowed to discount?

A: You can do whatever you want! Some companies do have an allowance for discounting. However, I'm a firm believer that discounting can be avoided. A discounting strategy — used poorly — can also see you lose trust. Recently, I engaged the services of a professional I'd never met before. They sent through their quote, which stated the cost would be $3300 for this work, but they would be happy to do it for $3000. This gave me the impression their first number was just made up. Fun fact: I ended up paying $2750. ☺

Gaining agreement

Once you've taken your prospect through objection handling, it's now simply a matter of steering the conversation towards their decision. In old-fashioned sales language, this would be called 'the close'. In modern-day sales language, you are simply going to present them with some collaborative questions — for example:

- So what would you like to do from here?

- It sounds to me like all your concerns are now out of the way, is that right?

- So are you happy to move things forward from here now?

- What are the steps from your end to formalise our agreement today?

Some friendly but direct questions such as these are much easier to present to someone to move your agreement forwards.

If at this point they agree to partner with you, then great! Congratulations, you've converted the opportunity — fist-bump! 🤜

Be sure to update your CRM that the opportunity has been 'closed' and 'won', and the close date is accurate. This is important so you can gather data and report on the length of your sales cycle — or, in other words, how long it takes you to convert opportunities.

If you don't get a 'yes' at the end of this meeting, all is certainly not lost. Let's keep playing ...

Playing the long game

As you have worked through the objection handling, your prospect might have some legitimate reasons why they can't move forward with you immediately. In this instance, you might feel you can't say or do anything to change their minds. Rest assured — this is completely acceptable. Sometimes other stars need to align before people can partner with you.

If you're selling in business to business (B2B) and your products or services carry a high ticket price, it would be unusual for someone to buy from you immediately at this stage of the process. In my business, as an example, no-one has ever bought from me in the first sales meeting, and fewer than 10 per cent of people buy from me in the second sales meeting.

Almost everyone I speak with is interested in our services, but almost everyone requires me to play some 'long game' with them until they are ready to proceed.

Some legitimate reasons you might not be able to overcome during your objection handling include:

- They need to recruit particular roles to allow your work together to succeed.

- They are about to kick off or wind down a major project.

- They need to financially account for your services in the next financial year.

I refer to situations such as these as you being put 'on ice'. They haven't said no to you; instead, it's more a case of 'not right now, but later on'. So you need to close off the meeting by asking permission to leave a door open.

I make the situation perfectly clear, and actually give prospects permission to say no to me, by telling them something like, 'That's completely fine if now isn't the right time — you can say no to me at any time!' ☺ To which they usually respond by clarifying they are not saying no, it's just a matter of time before they proceed.

I'll then invite them to stay in touch and ask if it would be okay for me to give them a call if I came across something that might be interesting to them. In 100 per cent of instances, they enthusiastically tell me of course they'd like to stay in touch.

This is where the fun (and the hard work) actually begins.

CHAPTER 9

STEP FIVE: FOLLOW UP

Many companies are doing sales by accident, and their approach to follow up is no different. They seem to send a proposal, and then cross their fingers and hope it converts. As I mentioned, hope is a terrible business strategy.

Did you know that in professional services, 90 per cent of new business contracts are converted *after* the point of sending a proposal? 90 per cent — that's almost *all* new business. But here's the disappointing news: only 44 per cent of people follow up proposals more than once.

So according to these numbers, the upside is that a whole lot of new business is out there for you to get, if you're willing to (surprise, surprise) follow the process, be disciplined and put in the effort.

Here are the three biggest reasons people do not follow up proposals:

1. They don't want to risk being annoying.

2. They don't know what to say.

3. They become caught in client delivery.

Let's be honest — who really likes to do things they aren't good at? No-one, surely! Once you know how to do follow-up correctly and collaboratively, this becomes an enjoyable experience for both yourself and your prospect.

The methodology I share in this chapter will help you shift the way you conduct your follow-up, so it becomes an activity you not only do, but also enjoy. This is because you're about to learn how to do follow-up in a way that doesn't make you annoying, but does allow you to serve and help others.

Knowing what *not* to do

Before I get into the guts of conducting follow-up, for the record, allow me to share what follow-up is not:

- *The 'Did you get my email?' email:* It goes like this:
  'Hi Melissa, I hope you're having a great week so far! I just wanted to check that you received my proposal last week and see if you have any questions.'

- *The 'Did you get my email?' voicemail:* It goes like this:
  'Hi Melissa, it's Julia here. I sent you that proposal last week and just wanted to see if you have any questions.'

- *The 'Did you get my email?' phone call:* It goes like this:
  'Hi Melissa! It's Julia here, how are you? That's great. How was your weekend? Are you having a good week so far? Great! Well, I just wanted to check that you received my email last week with my proposal and ask if you have any questions.'

I can confidently tell you three things about those enquiries:

1. Yes, Melissa did receive your email, because that's what happens when you send emails — people receive them.

2. No, Melissa doesn't have any questions, because if she did, she would have contacted you.

3. Contacting Melissa in any of these ways is not how you do follow-up in The Infinite Sales System. Leave that kind of follow-up for your competitors.

Value-adding follow-up

Wouldn't it be great if you had a genuinely great reason to contact your prospect, and that when you called them, they responded with enthusiasm? And as a nice by-product of your follow-up, you could build even more trust with your prospect and become a valuable member of their network?

This is what you should be aiming to do with follow-up. You're going to supercharge the process, so it's not just follow-up, but *value-adding* follow-up.

The race of 1000 competitors

The most common complaint I hear about follow-up is around prospects who don't reply to follow-up emails. But the problem isn't really with the prospects. Following up via email is a losing strategy where you're competing with too many others. I liken this to entering a running race. Would you rather enter a race of 1000 competitors, or a race of three competitors?

Your odds are incredibly low in the race of 1000 competitors — and this is the same as following up over email. I don't know about you, but my email has much more coming in than going out, and anyone emailing me asking for my business (or following up an opportunity) is likely to get pushed down the pile of competing priorities.

It's also important to note that if you are selling your services to CEOs or managing directors, like I am, people in these kinds of roles often have assistants managing their inbox, so your email will be not only lost among the many others coming in, but also perhaps not even seen by your prospect.

Plus, if you send the 'Did you get my email?' email and they don't reply, what's your next move? You can't very well email them *again* the next week with a 'Did you get the email I sent about asking you if you got my email?', can you? I feel like you get my point!

Your odds are significantly better in the race of three competitors — that is, where you're following up through making phone calls, which is what I recommend. You'll have much more successful cut through, and have frequent opportunities to build your relationship (and trust) with your prospect.

So, in case it wasn't clear, follow-up is not via email, and certainly not via text message. It's done by picking up the phone and having dialogue. And that dialogue is not simply asking if your prospect received your email and if they have any questions.

Time frame for following up

The general rule is if it's been three months since you've spoken to your prospect, it's been too long.

Using my CRM, I put in a follow-up task for 10 weeks after each time I speak with a prospect. This ensures no-one is ever forgotten, and forces me to keep in touch.

The reason I put the task in for 10 weeks in the future (rather than 12) is because when my CRM reminds me the task is due, I might not have a good enough reason to call the prospect, so I 'snooze' the task for a few days. I might do this a few times before they are really on my mind and I have thought hard enough and have eventually come up with a legitimate reason to contact them. So the extra couple of weeks in there give me a buffer so my contact doesn't blow out past three months.

Reasons to follow up

The key to successful follow-up is having an excellent reason to pick up the phone in the first place. If your reason isn't good enough, don't pick up the phone. Ideally, you want the reason for your follow-up phone call to be completely unrelated to your proposal or your desire to sell something. Your reason should be something that serves your prospect more than it serves you, and the more unrelated to your services it is, the more trust you will build.

As I've mentioned previously, no-one ever buys from me in a first sales meeting, and most don't buy in the second sales meeting either. So from the very beginning, I expect to need to follow up with prospects and play the long game. If you're selling in a business to business (B2B) world and your products or services are high-ticket items, you'll likely be in the same boat. Not being prepared with the same expectations is setting yourself up to fail and for disappointment.

Knowing I'll likely be playing the long game, I want to make it easier for myself right from the start.

> ## In the first sales meeting, I'm not only following the framework as I've already covered, but also sifting through all the information coming at me, looking and listening for any reason I might be able to call them in 10 weeks from now.

You can pick up the phone and contact a prospect you've not spoken to in a few months for many genuine value-adding reasons — but likely not the one you're thinking of. Whenever I ask about this in training sessions, one of the top answers people come up with is 'market or industry update'.

Generally, a market or industry update is *not* a good enough reason to contact a prospect. The only caveat to this is if you have market or industry information 'hot off the press' that you know for a fact your prospect will highly value. If your market or industry update is common knowledge or can be read about in the news, you're going to need a much better reason.

The other reason this is a terrible idea for a follow-up phone call is due to another barrier you're going to come up against. Your prospect has unlikely stored your contact information in their phone, so when you call them, you'll appear as a random number, which many people don't like answering. Or they might not be available at the time you call. So it's highly likely you'll be talking to their voicemail as your first point of contact. (But more on that in the next section.)

So what are some great reasons to pick up the phone? Here's a list to get you started:

- invite to an event

- invite to a webinar (you've seen or are attending)

- introduction to someone

- new project you've heard about they might be interested in

- make a referral

- provide new and exciting information

- ask for their help

- interview them for content for newsletter or podcast

- recommend a resource you've spoken about.

To expand on this list, I have a few 'go-to' follow-up reasons that I know bring great value to my prospects. The first one is if I'm going to a networking event, sundowner or other event, I'm always thinking about who I can invite to come along with me, because they will benefit from meeting the other attendees. If I'm going to a presentation, I'll again think about who might be interested in the content, and I usually bring at least one '+1' with me.

The second reason is I introduce them to someone who I know will benefit them. In fact, I'll go as far as saying I'm a serial introducer, and I'm always hooking up good people within my network. I have a sticky note on my computer with contacts in five trusted companies in my network whom I love to introduce to my prospects. I have an award writer (for prospects who want to win an award), a tender/bid writer, a marketer who specialises in innovation and sustainability, an expert at a tech platform for companies involved in tenders and bids, and a recruiter who uses creative ways to help recruit staff.

When my CRM alert pops up and reminds me to contact a particular prospect for follow-up, I go to my list and see who might be valuable for them to meet. My CRM will also have records of past contact, so I know who I have introduced them to previously.

My third go-to reason is asking for help. Now I know this isn't in line with your follow-up serving someone else (rather than yourself), but it is highly effective — and, I don't know about you, but when you're in business, you *always* need help or advice with something. So I look for opportunities to tap into my network and see who can help me with something topical. I'm also okay with being vulnerable and I know asking for help is necessary sometimes. As a bonus in this context, I've found that people love helping people, so there is a lot of benefit in asking for help.

In the past, I've followed up with prospects and asked them for help in recommending other service providers, or about how they may have solved a particular business problem. I might ask if they know someone who can help me, or even if they would be willing to introduce me to someone I'd like to meet.

When you get to talk with your prospect, let them know up-front the reason you're calling. This could be because:

- You crossed paths with someone who might be a useful introduction for them.

- You are attending an event and would like to invite them along, because some other attendees would likely be their core client-type.

- You saw (or attended) a webinar on a particular topic you know is important to them.

- You have a contact who is looking for the services they provide, and you'd like to introduce them.

- You came across a resource (or a book) that specifically covered a niche topic you had previously spoken about.

Your reason for contact must resonate with your prospect. If you think it's a bit 'loosey-goosey', then snooze your CRM task and put your thinking cap on for a few days until you come up with something better.

If you're clutching at straws, you can also take a look through their LinkedIn profile and look for topical prompts in what they may have posted about or commented on.

FAQ

Q: If you have this information, why can't you simply just email it through to them?

A: If you have a great reason to contact them and you email it, they may not see it or it may not be prioritised, because it's gotten lost in their inbox or someone else manages their emails. Importantly, if you email them your great reason, you don't get to have the dialogue!

Although I don't ask during the phone call, your prospect will often volunteer an update on your proposal, which is helpful for you to hear. It's also nice for you to be able to thank them for the update, and share it wasn't the reason you were calling. You finish the call, feeling good about helping someone, and then update your CRM to contact them again in 10 weeks with another reason.

By following this pattern, you're always sure to never lose touch with your prospects — and you get to build your network and reputation at the same time!

Voicemail messages

I'm frequently asked about voicemail and if you should leave a message when following up with a prospect, or just let the missed call be registered. My advice: leave a voicemail, but leave a good one. You want your prospect to return your call, and the quality of your voicemail will either have them call you back, or ignore you.

You message should be short and clear, but also intriguing or curious. It should also give an indication you are staying in touch. Here's what I use:

> *Hi there, Mohammed. Its Julia Ewert here. I crossed paths with someone who I think will be a great introduction for you. My number is* [add number]. *If I don't hear back from you by this afternoon, I'll try you again tomorrow after lunch.*

Your voicemail is not:

> *Hi there, Mohammed. It's Julia Ewert here. I crossed paths with Frazer Bradley recently from X company who I think could be a great introduction for you because I recall you were looking for someone in that industry. Anyway, I can introduce you if you like. My number is* [add number]. *Feel free to give me a call back when you have a chance!*

This gives them too much information and little reason to call you back, because they can decide without you if Frazer Bradley is useful or not. So you miss out on having some dialogue with them.

Follow up is designed to help you keep in touch, keep up your contact and serve your network. It's impossible to do this if you don't follow up, or think that email is going to get you there. It won't.

Follow the process. Just do the things.

The 'Are you dead?' email

I'm going to break the golden rule of follow-up here.

Up until now, I've been calling out, in neon lights, that you should never follow up over email. This strategy is the only one exception to that rule, but I warn you: use this sparingly.

When you really have tried all the options to get in touch with someone, you have one final, very effective, move you can try — which I call the 'Are you dead?' email. Because, surely, if you've tried all the things to get in touch and they aren't replying, they must be dead!

Plot twist: You're not actually going to ask them that!

When I expose this technique to my clients, it's always polarising. Half the room exclaim with shock and surprise and tell me they could never send this. The other half are completely on board, or at least open to trying it.

I can't take credit for inventing this technique, though; it comes from Chris Voss in his book *Never Split the Difference*.

The email goes like this:

Subject: *Have you given up?*

Email:

Hi/Dear [name],

I just wanted to ask if you've given up on your plans to [project summary]?

Kind regards,

Julia

The first time I used this, I had an exciting prospect who was saying all the right things and making all the right noises through my sales process. We had several, positive sales meetings, all within weeks. Then, all of a sudden, crickets.

I tried the various value-adding follow-up ideas I've covered in this chapter, but I couldn't get a sign of life. After about nine months, I thought it was time. Nervously, I typed out the email, exactly the way it was designed. Then hit send. And felt sick in my stomach. I didn't want to offend them, but it was my very last attempt to reach them because nothing else seemed to be working.

Within 10 minutes, I got a reply! They shared that they had not given up, but some internal priorities had changed so their sales training focus had to be pushed back.

I ended up winning that contract, and what was fascinating was that part of the team's curriculum was a module on follow-up, which incorporated this technique. As I got to this part in the session, the client who hired me piped up and shared with the group, in front of everyone: 'Julia, you used that on me. And I didn't like it.'

Knowing I had my muscle memory built-in with objection handling, I calmly responded, after a short pause, 'Oh, yes. Tell me more about that.'

My client went on to explain they didn't like this tactic because it was arrogant, and this wasn't how they had found me throughout the process previously. It was a bit of a shock to the system because it felt so different to the rest of our interactions.

Here's how the rest of the conversation went:

Me: [Pause] *So it seems you really hated it?*

Client: *Yes! I'm not someone who gives up!*

Me: *And it sounds like you thought it was very arrogant, but you don't think I'm arrogant, is that right?*

Client: *Yes!*

Me: [With a slow smile] *And yet, ... here I am.*

To which my client laughed, as did the rest of the team — who were on the edge of their seats (with their popcorn) watching this interaction!

I went on to explain that this technique is designed to be exactly that — a circuit breaker to get their attention. It's meant to be a bit of a 'sledgehammer' among the process.

This technique is also designed to appeal to the human inclination that most of us have — that is, not wanting to be known as someone who gives up. So, in most cases, people reply with a justification of sorts, as to their current status of your project or conversation.

This same session happened to also include the company's head of marketing, who chimed in with a suggestion that the wording of this technique wasn't very 'on-brand' for their company's 'tone of voice'. They said that if they were going to use this kind of email as their last resort, they might re-word it to sound something like the following:

Dear [name]*,*

I hope you are well.

Thank you so much over the past while for your interest in [project summary]*. It's been great to learn about you and to be able to provide some suggestions for how we could help.*

We've been trying to reach you lately, and wanted to let you know we'd still love to help you if you'd like to let us know how we can do so.

Our offices are open and we'd love to invite you in again so we can discuss how we can help you with [project summary]*.*

Have a lovely day and I hope to hear from you soon.

Now, I don't know about you, but that email seems an entire planet away from the original one.

So I offered a different perspective, and emphasised that my original email is designed to be different. Even though it's not even my technique, I've had a huge amount of success from using it, on the rare occasions I've need to. I advised against changing the email to their version, because if the prospect isn't replying to them, and they have tried all the things to get in touch, then they have probably already tried that kind of email — and it hasn't worked.

This technique works, because it is different. It's abrupt, and perhaps a little bit arrogant. Changing it would make it a different technique. Don't mess with the system. Keep it simple. Just do the things.

In all the years, I've known about this technique, if I've used it even a dozen times, I'd be surprised. And, in every instance, with the exception of one, I've received a reply, so the strike rate of success if pretty high. I wouldn't want to mess with that!

FAQ

Q: How long do you wait before pulling this email out?

A: Well, the short answer is, 'It depends'. There are too many variables. What I can share is that you need to be absolutely certain this is the end of the line and you've tried everything else on the planet to get this person's attention. If I had to put a time to it, I would suggest you'd be getting close to a year of no contact, and several attempts at value-adding follow-up.

The doughnut card

Years ago, I had a first sales meeting with a prospect and they were super enthusiastic about my services. They told me they wanted to have this locked and loaded within four weeks. Referring back to a phrase I used back in chapter 5, I had 'happy ears' like you wouldn't believe!

Now, given this story appears in the 'follow-up' section of this book, what do you think happened? I'll tell you — a lot of not much!

We booked in the second sales conversation and they were still telling me all the right things to suggest they would move forward. Then a third sales meeting ... And then they didn't want to book another meeting, but just wanted me to leave it with them. I conducted a few successful value-adding follow-up calls over the coming months, and then they disappeared into the ether.

What I didn't know was happening in the background was that they were going through a major business restructure to set themselves up for taking the company public. This meant that implementing a sales process wasn't as high on their priority list as I originally thought.

After many months of trying to get in touch with them, to no avail, I thought maybe it was time to deploy the 'Are you dead?' email. I felt like I'd tried everything else. Knowing this email was the end of the line, however, I thought long and hard about using it, and ended up deciding there must still be another way I could get in touch. My key contact was based on the other side of the country, so I couldn't very well just swing by their office and see if they were in.

Side point: I have also done the swing-by-and-pop-in in the past!

I cared about this opportunity and really wanted to help them, so I decided there must be another way. Nearby where I live is a really funky bookshop that also has an excellent range of greeting cards, so I decided to send the prospect a card in the post. I know — a handwritten card in the post! How old-fashioned, I hear you exclaim!

I saw a card with doughnuts on it and thought this was the one. Because who doesn't like doughnuts? No-one, that's who! (Right? If I'm not right, I don't want to hear it.)

On the inside, I wrote a message along the lines of:

Hi there Jaxon,

It's been a while since we've spoken and I've been trying to reach you. When we first met, you mentioned you wanted to have this all tied up in four weeks, so I wonder if I've misunderstood something along the way.

Also, I wanted to be cheeky enough to ask if I could exchange these paper doughnuts for a sign of life — you've been hard to catch!

Anyway, it would be great to pick up the contact again,

Kind regards,

Julia

And within a few weeks, I got a call and was back in the game! All it took was a little creative thinking. I went back to that shop and stocked up on all their doughnut cards — and also the ones with cupcakes, fairy bread and even some with sushi on the front! Just in case I needed them in the future.

Interestingly, over the years, I've only needed to send another card like this maybe three times, because all the other follow-up ideas continue to work.

Let me ask you — what's your 'doughnut card' equivalent?

 What's something you can do that reflects effort and is aligned with your personality?

Trust the process

I recall a conversation with another professional (not a client), who shared they were finding sales hard and that one prospect in particular just wasn't replying to them. I asked what they were doing to try to get in touch. They said they were trying everything — which, after a few more questions, they clarified to mean they had sent a bunch of 'Did you get my email?' emails.

So, in fact, they'd tried nothing.

The point here is if you care about the opportunity and you want to convert it, you need to try all the things. If you're not bothered about converting it, then try very little or even nothing at all.

When I have a genuinely great reason to call a prospect for follow up, I look forward to making the phone call. It's a great chance to offer them something, and I'm almost always rewarded with some nice dialogue and an opportunity to catch up again, so the process keeps moving forward.

Through value-adding follow-up, not only have I won truckloads of new clients, but many of these prospects have become professional friends (before becoming clients) because they see true value in me as a professional. These follow-up calls also give us both further reasons to connect and find things in common, which makes me even more trustworthy.

This part of the sales process never ends, because if you are continually conducting first sales meetings, eventually those prospects will move through the process to the follow-up stage, and you might find it takes four, six or even 15 follow-up calls to finally win the business.

  One of the most fulfilling parts of follow-up is that even those prospects who never end up converting often still become great contacts, and even friends, so you're still rewarded.

CHAPTER 10

PUTTING THE PROCESS TOGETHER

Congratulations! You now have all the pieces of The Infinite Sales System to get you going!

Let me put the complete puzzle together for you, so you know how all the pieces go together.

STEP ONE: Qualification process

Embedded into your 'contact us' form

OR

Sent over email, prior to booking in your first Sales Meeting

OR

Asked over the phone when enquiry comes in

STEP TWO: The first sales meeting

CHITCHAT
Share something personal

↓

4-STEP AGENDA
I'd like to respect your time ...

↓

OPEN QUESTIONS
Tell me about ...

↓

SUMMARY
If I've understood correctly, it appears as though ...

↓

I CAN HELP YOU
I want to let you know that I can help you solve this ...

↓

EMOTIONAL BENEFITS
Although it's a [vehicle], what you're really buying when you partner with us is ...

↓

RECOMMENDATIONS
1. Technical questions
2. Here are our services
3. Here's some initial thoughts
4. I'll send you a proposal

↓

NEXT STEPS
Let's make a time for us to have a chat again so that we can keep the momentum going on our conversation.
I've got my calendar handy, do you have yours?

STEP THREE: Meeting follow up

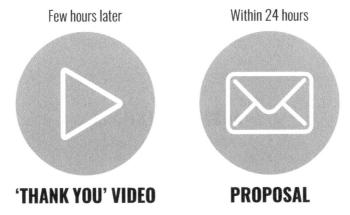

Few hours later   Within 24 hours

'THANK YOU' VIDEO   **PROPOSAL**

STEP FOUR: The second sales meeting

OPEN
What did you make of our conversation the other day?

ANSWER QUESTIONS
What would you like to ask?

OBJECTION HANDLING
· Acknowledge
· Clarify
· Shopping list
· Confirm
· Solutions

CLOSE
Does that help you to be more comfortable now
with what we have recommended?

'YES' OR 'YES SOON'
Move forward with contract,
next meeting etc.

FOLLOW UP
Value-adding contact,
CRM 'tasks'

STEP FIVE: Follow up

FOLLOW UP

Value-adding ⟶ CRM ⟶ 'Are you dead?' ⟶ The doughnut ⟶ Trust the
contact   'tasks'   email   card   process

CRM usage

Remember — your CRM is designed to help not hinder you, so be sure to put all your steps in as you go and, importantly, keep those regular tasks being created for your three monthly contact. You don't want any of your new and valuable contacts to slip through your fingers after all your hard work so far!

CONCLUSION

The Infinite Sales System is specifically designed for you — the person who doesn't love doing sales and may not even be in a full-time sales position. It allows you to simply be yourself.

If you do nothing, nothing changes. Like any new skill, this sales process takes practice and patience to get right. Don't give in. More importantly, don't go back to using old-school, outdated sales tactics and tricks.

You deserve better.

In particular, keep the following in mind as you start your journey.

Sales with humility

You can simply be yourself through this process. There is zero requirement for you to overhaul your personality and become a raging extrovert. This process is designed so you can help your prospect to feel valued and heard by making *them* the centre of the conversation. You'll be there, open-minded, and ready to listen and learn.

Trust-first approach

By approaching each new prospect with high-quality open questions, you'll build connection and likeability like never before, and your conversations will be more enjoyable and fruitful. The process will feel better this way, because you'll be forming genuine relationships and long-lasting partnerships.

Human connection

Through being humble and focusing on trust first, you'll build a huge network of trusted, valuable and friendly connections. Business will be fun.

Remember: revenue = sales = business.

A final phrase for you to take away:

Keep it simple.
Just do the things.

ADDITIONAL RESOURCES FOR CONTINUAL LEARNING

The individual skills within The Infinite Sales System require continual practice in order to refine. As Tony Robbins highlights, 'Repetition is the mother of skill', so here are some ways to continue your learning and move towards true mastery:

- *Sign up to receive my monthly Smart Sales publication:* I share case studies and topical examples showing how to apply the sales and negotiation skills in The Infinite Sales System. Just go to juliaewert.com/sign-up-for-smart-sales-newsletter or use the QR code.

- *Follow me on LinkedIn via Julia Ewert MBA, FAIM:* I post regularly about skills, techniques, stories, mistakes and tips, all designed to help you improve. Send me a connection request, and don't forget to attach a message saying hello! I love hearing from people who have read my book! I also love hearing about any sales wins you've had or stories of success, so please get in touch.

- *Contact me directly via info@juliaewert.com:* You can ask other FAQs or, again, share wins and stories. You can even share any tips you have for me — perhaps you've found your own version of the doughnut card!

If you'd like to benefit from having The Infinite Sales System customised and implemented across your organisation, please contact me via my website — juliaewert.com/contact/ — and we can arrange for an informal conversation about how it can work for you.

Please share with others that you've read this book. Remember not to give them your copy — by now, it should be full of notes, scribbles and pages turned down! Help me spread the word that there is a modern-day way to do sales!

Thank you for being here with me.

Printed and bound by CPI Group (UK) Ltd, Croydon, CR0 4YY

19/06/2024